NOTTINGHAM'S MILITARY LEGACY

GERRY VAN TONDER

Pen & Sword
MILITARY

First published in Great Britain in 2017 by
PEN AND SWORD MILITARY
an imprint of
Pen and Sword Books Ltd
47 Church Street
Barnsley
South Yorkshire S70 2AS

Copyright © Gerry van Tonder, 2017

ISBN 978 1 52670 758 1

Typeset by Aura Technology and Software Services, India
Maps, drawings and militaria in the colour section by Colonel Dudley Wall
Printed and bound in Malta by Gutenberg Press Ltd

Pen & Sword Books Ltd incorporates the imprints of Pen & Sword
Archaeology, Atlas, Aviation, Battleground, Discovery, Family History, History, Maritime,
Military, Naval, Politics, Railways, Select, Social History, Transport, True Crime, Claymore Press,
Frontline Books, Leo Cooper, Praetorian Press, Remember When, Seaforth Publishing and Wharncliffe.

For a complete list of Pen and Sword titles please contact
Pen and Sword Books Limited
47 Church Street, Barnsley, South Yorkshire, S70 2AS, England
email: enquiries@pen-and-sword.co.uk
website: www.pen-and-sword.co.uk

CONTENTS

Captain Albert Ball VC, DSO & Two Bars, MC, memorial, Nottingham Castle. (Photo Gerry van Tonde

INTRODUCTION

> The willingness with which our young people are likely to serve in any war, no matter how justified, shall be directly proportional to how they perceive veterans of early wars were treated and appreciated by our nation.
>
> George Washington

Commander-in-chief of the Continental Army during the American fight for self-determination, and the new nation's first head of state, the name of George Washington and everything that it stands for, is permanently and irrevocably memorialized in the American psyche, his legacy enshrined in stone and bronze.

In no different manner, material reminders track Nottingham and the county's much-repeated answer to the call of the colours over many centuries.

For so many of us, the names Robin Hood and Sherwood Forest conjure up images of legendary heroes and fabulous places, which have not only become romanticized and immortalized in the heady realms of the silver screen, but are also inherent threads in the fabric of Nottingham and the nation's folklore.

Robin Hood of lore, Nottingham Castle. (Photo Gerry van Tonder)

An ancient unwritten mantra of 'fighting the good fight' for a noble cause, especially when applied to foreign conflicts or disorder, would cause many an able-bodied man to take the king's shilling. Nowhere was this more evident than in the Great War, when large tracts of Nottinghamshire, overnight, were suddenly without men and boys, gone to give the Kaiser a bloody nose.

But gone also was the challenge and joy of an adventure that would be over by Christmas, to be replaced by empty beds, homes and villages as thousands upon thousands failed to return. For many left behind, there could never be closure. It was determined by the Imperial War Graves Commission that the mortal remains of British soldiers would not be repatriated to Britain for burial, but be interred in largely 'concentrated' military cemeteries in the sovereign lands where they had fought. The greatest tragedy, however, was the imponderably large numbers of soldiers whose bodies were never found, their final places of rest only 'known unto God'.

Their legacy of an unquestioned loyalty that saw them, at the shrill blast of a whistle, scramble 'over the top' with not a moment's hesitation, was immediately established as they charged into the slaughter of no man's land. A nation numbed with shock will, however, also talk of its brave sons.

A military legacy is, more often than not, far less tangible. Individually or combined, individuals, entities and places in time contribute in equal measure to that which is remembered collectively, including events that history would prefer to overlook.

Since ancient times, Britain suffered invasion from continental Europe: Germanic Saxons, Vikings, Normans – Spain, France and Germany also had designs on the island. Such invasions were rarely passive. Invariably, civil instability created by the arrival of the Europeans allowed opportunistic usurpers to established kingdoms and fiefdoms to take up arms to achieve their ends.

This all required men at arms, essential for both deterrent and belligerent purposes. This would usually take the form of civilian volunteers who would be available to take up arms when called upon to do so. This in itself nurtured an evolving legacy – mercenaries, knights, bands, regiments of foot and horse, militia, yeomanry, to the more recent identity of territorial forces.

With time, these military structures became more formal in structure, necessitated by intermittent internal crises, from riotous civil unrest to armed insurrection against the Crown. In the case of the latter, the worst scenario was civil war, in which the very divisive nature of the conflict prevented the formation of a national, all-encompassing and omnipotent military loyal to the king or queen of the day.

Thirteenth-century settlement of a dispute.

The demands for the defence of a burgeoning global empire, which had become Britain's source of enormous wealth, would provide the military cohesion that the emerging trade and industrial giant required.

Britain, however, quickly discovered that it was not the only ambitious player on the international stage. Conflict was therefore inevitable, initially for control of the resources needed to sustain a healthy economy, and later by the indigenous owners of such resources who felt that their wealth was being plundered at their expense. The East Indies, Afghanistan, South Africa, America, China and the Indian sub-continent placed a great strain on the British armed forces.

It was also a time when a great emphasis started to be placed on the brave exploits of Britain's men in uniform in their defence of the Crown's realm. A national collective legacy started to develop, greatly assisted by significant advances in communication, especially through newspapers. A plethora of latter-day Robin Hood-styled heroes arose in the minds of the nation – the unprecedented gallant defence of Rorke's Drift by a handful of Redcoats against waves of vastly superior numbers of Zulu warriors. Eleven of these men would be awarded the Victoria Cross – they became legend. The legacy of this singular victory would, however, largely screen the ignominious and costly failure at Isandlwana the previous day.

The Anglo-Boer War followed twenty years later, during which the need to draw on the legacy-based propaganda of British armed invincibility was even more profound.

The Great War hurt most. People at home struggled to compute the numbers of fatalities that were daily thrust upon them.

ʳim determination on the face of the Second World War British soldier. (Photo *The War Illustrated*)

First World War memorial bronze, St Mary's Church, Nottingham. (Photo Gerry van Tonder)

As the guns on the Western Front fell silent after four years, and the Armistice signed the outpouring of national grief and pride dictated that the legacy of both slaughter and bravery will never be allowed to be forgotten. Churches, cemeteries, civil buildings, villages towns and cities erected lasting symbols of memorial to a generation lost in the Great War.

Rudyard Kipling, having lost his 18-year-old son Jack, listed as 'missing' in France, chose the epitaph for architect Lutyens's Stone of Remembrance found in all Commonwealth War Graves Commission cemeteries: 'Their Name Liveth For Evermore'.

Britain's fallen during the Second World War would be remembered in the same man-ner, and since then, the Armed Forces Memorial at the National Memorial Arboretum is custodian of the legacy.

Throughout Nottinghamshire, communities laud their uniformed heroes, both those who lost their lives in the theatres of conflict and those whose bravery in combat make them forever proud.

In these pages, a thread is followed through time that feeds the legacy of a city and county's military history. The trail is holistic, with fleeting glances of some of the people units, conflicts and places that contributed to Nottingham's military inheritance.

1. A BRIEF HISTORY

1068
A contemporary chronicle reports that William of Normandy 'went to Nottingham and built a castle there'. At the time, the king was en route to Yorkshire to quell an insurrection in the area.

1194
Upon his return from one of his crusades, Richard I, 'the Lionheart', laid siege to Nottingham Castle in which the rebellious Prince John and his supporters had ensconced themselves. The castle's occupants surrendered within days.

1461
While combating Lancastrians in the English midlands, Edward IV, of the House of York, proclaims himself king in Nottingham, effectively using the castle as a military stronghold.

Nottingham Castle mural.
(Photo Gerry van Tonder)

9

1485

Tudor Henry VII defeats Richard's Yorkist forces at the Battle of Bosworth Field, and proclaims himself king 'by right of conquest'. More out of necessity, the new monarch retains Nottingham Castle as a royal fortress.

1536

Henry VIII, following the introduction of Dissolution of the Lesser Monasteries Act of this year, deals ruthlessly with rebel leaders who are fomenting resistance to the king's church reforms. As a result of the threat, Henry significantly bolsters the Nottingham Castle garrison.

22 August 1642

Charles I raises his royal standard outside Nottingham Castle as a rallying point for those loyal to the Crown, signalling, many believe, the start of the Civil War.

Finding divided loyalties in the town, the monarch leaves for Shrewsbury to drum up more support. In his absence, Parliamentarian forces under Colonel John Hutchinson garrison the castle.

September 1643

A 600-strong contingent of Royalist troops are unsuccessful in their attempt to retake the castle. The Parliamentarians retain possession until the end of the war.

1649

Charles I is found guilty of treason and executed, and to prevent Nottingham Castle from again being used as a royal stronghold, the keep and the fortifications of the upper bailey are demolished under orders from John Hutchinson.

1741

In pursuance of orders from George II for the raising of seven new infantry regiments, the 56th Regiment of Foot is formed, titled Houghton's Regiment of Foot after the regiment's first commanding officer, Colonel Daniel Houghton.

1748

The 56th is renumbered the 45th Regiment of Foot and retitled Warburton's Regiment of Foot.

1750

The 45th is now stationed in Nova Scotia.

1755

Threat of a renewed war with France sees the raising of the Nottinghamshire 59t Regiment of Foot.

The 45th forms part of a 2,000-strong expedition to oust the French at Fort Beau Sejou at the head of the Bay of Fundy, on the north-east coast of Atlantic Canada.

1751

The regiment's title is simplified to the 45th Regiment of Foot.

1755

The 45th Regiment of Foot is shipped to Canada to do battle with the French to gain control of that part of North America. Three years later, the regiment earns its first battle honours at Louisbourg, a decisive victory in the French and Indian War.

The 45th returns to England, its strength barely 100 men.

1772

The 59th is stationed in Boston, Massachusetts when the American War of Independence beaks out. The regiment suffers heavy casualties.

1782

Authority is granted for the regiment to be retitled the 45th (1st Nottinghamshire) Foot.

The 59th is posted to Gibraltar for ten years, at which time their county designation is incorporated into the regiment's title: 59th (2nd Nottinghamshire) Regiment of Foot.

1786

The 45th is posted to the West Indies, where disease severely depletes their numbers, returning to England and their base at Chatham in 1801.

1794

The Nottinghamshire Yeomanry Cavalry is raised.

The 59th forms part of the British force deployed to Flanders during the war with France.

painting by an unknown artist of French and British ships of the line engaging in a critical naval attle during the American War of Independence at Chesapeake Bay in September 1781.

1795

After evacuation from the continent, the 59th sails for the West Indies for a seven-year tour of duty.

1804

A second battalion of the 45th is raised in Mansfield, Nottinghamshire.

In August, a second battalion of the 59th is formed, which remains in England on garrison duty, while the 1st Battalion leaves for the Cape of Good Hope, where the battalion earns its first battle honour against the Dutch.

1807

The 45th, numbering 892 NCOs and men, is part of a large second British expedition that arrives in Argentina to wrest Montevideo and Buenos Aires from the Spanish. The British suffer a humiliating defeat in the streets of Buenos Aires, sustaining massive casualties in conditions best described as urban combat. Lieutenant General John Whitelocke capitulates, and leaving 400 seriously wounded men behind, clears all British forces from Buenos Aires and Montevideo and sails home. He is subsequently court-martialled and cashiered.

1808

The 59th's 2nd Battalion leaves for duty on the Iberian Peninsula.

1808–15

During the Napoleonic Wars, the 45th Regiment of Foot fights with Sir Arthur Wellesley's army against the French in the Iberian Peninsula, where the regiment remains for six years. The regiment's strength stands at 35 officers and 732 other ranks.

1812

The 2nd Battalion, the 59th, returns to Spain, and later participates in several major battles such as Vitoria, Nivelle and the Nive.

6 April 1812

The 45th acquits itself gallantly during the storming of the castle at Badajoz, a feat celebrated to this day by the Mercian Regiment, and known as Badajoz Day. (see Chapter 3)

1816

The 2nd Battalion, the 59th is disbanded, and the 1st Battalion is retitled the 59th (2nd Nottinghamshire) Regiment of Foot.

1819

The 45th is posted to Ceylon, where headquarters is set up in Colombo and tours of duty conducted in Burma and India.

1823

In anticipation of a second war with the French, more regiments are raised, and the 95th Regiment of Foot is formed. Two years later, it is titled the 95th (Derbyshire) Foot.

1843

In April, the 45th arrives in the Cape, South Africa, to address various issues, including slavery, unrest among indigenous ethnic groups and itinerant Dutch farmers. A detachment is sent to the convict station on Robben Island, the future place of incarceration of South African freedom activist, Nelson Mandela.

Two companies of the 45th are deployed to Natal, where a garrison is established at Pietermaritzburg.

1848

The 'district' between the Orange and Vaal rivers, is proclaimed the 'Orange River Sovereignty' by Britain, precipitating immediate dissent from the migrant Dutch who had already settled in the territory.

Two companies of the 45th, together with elements of the Cape Mounted Rifles and the Royal Artillery, garrison Bloemfontein.

1849

The 59th participates in the First Opium War with the Qing Dynasty in China.

1858

In January, the 59th, together with elements from the Royal Marine Light Infantry and the Royal Navy, occupy the Chinese city of Canton.

1859

The 45th arrive back home. According to Colonel Philip Dalbiac:

> weak in numbers, many of the men having been left behind as settlers. The men who returned wore their beards and their bronzed, hardy, and workmanlike appearance as they marched out of Portsmouth Dockyard which won the admiration of all beholders.

30 May 1859

The 1st Nottinghamshire Rifle Volunteer Force, dubbed the Robin Hood Rifles by Nottingham's mayoress, holds its first drill on the East Terrace of Nottingham Castle.

1864

The 45th returns to India.

1866

The 45th is granted Royal authority to include 'Sherwood Foresters' in its title:

> Horse Guards, S.W.,
> 12th December, 1866.
> Major-General Drought,
> Colonel of the 45th (Nottinghamshire Regiment), 'Sherwood Foresters.'
>
> Sir
> With reference to your letter of the 7th ultimo forwarding an application from the officer commanding the 45th or Nottinghamshire regiment, of which you are the colonel,

I am desired by the field-marshal commanding-in-chief to inform you that, on the recommendation of His Royal Highness, Her Majesty has been graciously pleased to approve of the regiment bearing in future the title of 'Sherwood Foresters,' with reference to the traditions of the county of Nottingham and in consideration of the regiment's distinguished services.

I have the honour to be, Sir,

Your obedient servant
(signed) T. Trowbridge, D.A.G.

1867

The 59th is posted to India and Ceylon for eleven years.

1868

An expeditionary force, commanded by Sir Robert Napier and including the 45th, arrives in the Horn of Africa to attend to rebel insurrection in Ethiopia and Abyssinia.

1872

After returning to their headquarters in Madras, the 45th is deployed to Burma once more.

1873

Under the Cardwell localization scheme, the 59th is brigaded with the 30th (Cambridgeshire) Regiment of Foot.

1878

The 45th returns to England.

With the situation between Russia and Turkey becoming increasingly volatile, Britain mobilizes her reserves, resulting in some 600 reservists from the Nottingham and Leicester regiments of militia joining the 45th, bringing its strength to 1,400.

The 59th crosses into Afghanistan from India as part of an expeditionary force to neutralize Russian influence in the territory. The regiment fights in the Battle of Ahmed Khel. (see Chapter 3)

1879

Following the devastating slaughter by the Zulu of 1,300 men of Lord's Chelmsford's force at Isandlwana at the end of January, eighty volunteers from the 45th are seconded to the 58th (Rutlandshire) Regiment of Foot and join an expedition headed for Natal.

1881

The outcome of Secretary of State for War Edward Cardwell's reforms of the military in Britain between 1868 and 1874, and continued by his successor, Hugh Childers, sees the 45th (Nottinghamshire) and the 95th (Derbyshire) regiments of foot amalgamated and titled The Sherwood Foresters.

Titled The Derbyshire Regiment (Sherwood Foresters) in May, two months later the regiment is retitled The Sherwood Foresters (Derbyshire Regiment).

On 2 July, the 45th ceases to exist. The '45' shoulder titles are replaced with the word 'Derb

Final demise of the Zulu nation at Ulundi, July 1879. (Source *Recent British Battles*)

The 59th (2nd Nottinghamshire) Regiment of Foot is amalgamated with the 30th (Cambridgeshire) Regiment of Foot to form The East Lancashire Regiment.

1882
The Sherwood Foresters first see action in Egypt.

1897
The Sherwood Foresters are deployed as part of the Tirah Expedition on the Indian North West Frontier.

1899–1902
The Anglo-Boer War sees mounted and foot infantry from the Sherwood Foresters shipped to South Africa.

The South Nottinghamshire Hussars see active service on the sub-continent.

Following an appeal by royal warrant for volunteers from the standing Yeomanry regiments, in 1900, the Nottinghamshire Yeomanry provides the 10th (Sherwood Rangers) Company for service in South Africa.

In 1902, The Sherwood Foresters (Derbyshire Regiment) is redesignated The Sherwood Foresters (Nottinghamshire and Derbyshire Regiment), more commonly referred to as Notts and Derby.

1908
The Robin Hood Rifles become the 7th (Robin Hood) Battalion, Sherwood Foresters.

First World War

The 7th (Robin Hood) Battalion, 17th (Welbeck Rangers) Battalion, and 15th (Nottingham) Battalion, Sherwood Foresters, the latter as a bantam battalion, are territorial units from Nottingham that see action on the Western Front.

The standing army element of the Sherwood Foresters contribute two front line and two reserve battalions.

The South Notts Hussars serve in Egypt, Gallipoli, Macedonia, Palestine and France.

The first line 1st Battalion, The Sherwood Rangers, serves in the Nottinghamshire and Derbyshire Mounted Brigade in Egypt as cavalry.

Second World War

The 150th (South Notts Hussars) Field Regiment, Royal Artillery, the 107th (South Notts Hussars) Regiment, Royal Horse Artillery (RHA), and the 107th (MED) Regiment, South Notts Hussars (TA), Royal Artillery (RA), see active service during the war.

1939

The Sherwood Rangers, continuing as a cavalry unit, are posted to the 5th Cavalry Brigade in Palestine.

M3A3 Grant tank used by Lieutenant General Bernard Montgomery, Eighth Army Commander, Western Desert campaign. (Photo Gerry van Tonder)

1940

The Robin Hoods relocate to the Royal Engineers and are transferred to the Royal Artillery.

The Sherwood Rangers convert to artillery, taking part in the defence of Tobruk and Benghazi.

1941

The Sherwood Rangers convert to armour, serving with the 8th Armoured Brigade where they operate Grant, Sherman and Crusader tanks in Eighth Army tank battles in the Western Desert, including at El Alamein. (see Chapter 3)

1944

The Sherwood Rangers land on the Normandy beaches on D-Day, with Duplex Drive (DD) Sherman and Sherman Firefly tanks.

With the demand for British infantry high, the 150th (South Notts Hussars) Field Regiment is disbanded.

1947

The 107th (South Notts Hussars) Regiment, Royal Horse Artillery and the 150th (South Notts Hussars) Field Regiment, become the 307th (RHA) (South Nottinghamshire Hussars Yeomanry) Field Regiment, RA and the 350th (South Nottinghamshire Hussars Yeomanry) Heavy Regiment, RA, respectively.

The 350th later merges into 350 (Robin Hood Foresters) Light Regiment, RA. The 307th continues as a battery in the present day Reserve Force, part of the 100th (Yeomanry) Regiment Royal Artillery.

1961

The Sherwood Rangers become a reconnaissance unit, equipped initially with Ferret and Alvis Saladin armoured cars, and later with Saracen and Sultan armoured personnel carriers (APC).

28 February 1970

The Sherwood Foresters merges with the Worcestershire Regiment to form the Worcestershire and Sherwood Foresters (WFR), comprising one regular (1WFR) and one territorial (3FR) battalion. They adopt the moniker 'the Woofers'.

1972

The 1st Battalion WFR is deployed to Northern Ireland.

1987

Elements of the WFR serve in Cyprus as part of the UN peacekeeping force.

1988

A second WFR territorial (TA) battalion, 4WFR is raised.

1992

The 4th Battalion WFR is disbanded after the fall of the Berlin Wall.

The Sherwood Rangers become B Squadron, The Queen's Own Yeomanry, tasked with reconnaissance duties for the Allied Command Europe (ACE) Rapid Reaction Corps.

Ferret scout car. (Photo Gerry van Tonder)

1996 and 1998

In accordance with the Dayton Peace Agreement, the Woofers perform two NATO peace keeping tours in Bosnia, codenamed Operation Resolute.

1999

B Squadron, The Queen's Own Yeomanry (formerly The Sherwood Rangers), re-joins the Royal Yeomanry as reserves on the FV4034 Challenger 2, a British main battle tank (MBT).

2005

The regiment is deployed to Afghanistan's Helmund Province under the auspices of NATO to assist with the facilitation of redevelopment.

2006

The Challenger 2 Yeomanry reserves are converted to CBRN reconnaissance: chemical, biological, radiological or nuclear warfare (including terrorism). More recently, the squadron is converted to light cavalry, equipped with the WMIK (weapons mounted installation kit) Land Rover Wolf variant.

1 September 2007

The Woofers are retitled the 2nd Battalion, The Mercian Regiment. The regiment is on a tour of duty in Helmund Province at the time. Concurrent with this reorganization, the 22nd Cheshire Regiment and the Staffordshire Regiment also merge, as 1st and 3rd battalions respectively.

2014

The 3rd Mercian (The Staffords) is absorbed by the other battalions, resulting in the formation of two battalions and a reserve battalion: 1st, 2nd and 4th Mercian. The new entity is titled The Mercian Regiment (Cheshires, Worcestershire and Sherwood Foresters, and Staffords). The regiment adopts the motto, 'Stand Firm, Strike Hard'.

2. CALL TO ARMS: HOME

> . . . for all the world knows that I never did begin a war with the two houses of Parliament. And I call on God to witness – to whom I must shortly make an account – that I never did intend for to encroach on their privileges.
>
> Charles I on his execution scaffold, Tuesday, 30 January 1649

The First English Civil War 1642

On 22 August 1642, frustrated by irreconcilable political differences at the seat of the nation's power and authority, Charles I formally declared war on his own parliament by raising his royal standard just outside Nottingham Castle, on what is today known as Standard Hill.

For some time, dissatisfaction with the Crown had been simmering in England, no less so in the Midlands counties of Nottingham, Derby and Leicester. Already embittered by the monarch's unpalatable religious reforms, Charles's unilateral introduction of stringent taxes resulted in open defiance and incidents in which the Crown's agents were assaulted in public.

Charles, however, lacked the military muscle to impose his will on a population that had rapidly become polarized.

In July, Charles toured the English midlands, to some extent to canvass support, but primarily to access war materiel from various county vaults and armouries. In April, his bid to seize a national stock of arms at Hull failed, his ships blocked from entering the port. After a similarly fruitless expedition to Leicester, Charles turned to Nottingham where, in the town hall at Weekday Cross, there was a repository of weaponry for local 'territorial forces known as Trained Bands.

Civil War re-enactment. (Courtesy Colonel Dudley Wall)

Charles sent his Lord Lieutenant, Lord Newark, and the County High Sheriff into the town, where, in the absence of the Nottingham Lord Lieutenant, an acrimonious argument ensued with Colonel John Hutchinson and Mayor John James over right of access to the town's magazine. Hutchinson, a Puritan leader, was a senior Parliamentarian officer. Six years later, his would also be one of fifty-nine signatures appended to Charles I's death warrant.

By way of compromise, two padlocks were affixed to the magazine door, with the high sheriff and the town mayor as dual key holders. Ultimately, however, it was an exercise in futility. On 19 August, just before Charles's momentous raising of his standard, a party of Royalists took an axe to the door. Three days later, the king arrived in Nottingham after having been equally unsuccessful at gaining access to the arms and ammunition store in Coventry.

Soon afterwards, the commander of Parliamentarian forces in the Midlands, Sir John Gell, took neighbouring Derby on behalf of Parliament, further allowing him to bolster Parliamentarian force strengths under Hutchinson at Nottingham:

[From Chesterfield] we presently marched to Wirksworth, drove [Sir Francis] Wortley and the crew out of the county, and then went straight to Derby; when our sudden appearing prevented the designs of our malignant countrymen, for whilst they were consulting how to raise forces to oppose us, and sharing every man's proportion, how many to maintain our being at Derby, in the midst of them crossed all, what could not be done by force, they then endeavoured to effect by [peaceful means], desiring the Colonel to give them meeting, but to leave his strength behind, a request too simple for us to yield unto.

Sir George Gresley was now joined with us, the only Gentleman of quality in this county, that cordially appeared to be on our side. Wortley returned into the Peake again, whom we suddenly sent away packing, with such a fear, that he troubled us no more.

Our neighbours at Nottingham were now desirous to raise some forces, which good work we were willing to advance, gave Captain White to go with his dragoons to them, who at first came to us with about 40 and went from us with about 100, well-armed.

(An extract from a contemporary document, Derbyshire County Records Office. Period spelling has been modernized.)

For the antagonists in the conflict, Newark, situated as it was on the Great North Road north-east of Nottingham, was of significant strategic importance. A mercenary from Scotland, Sir John Henderson, had assisted Royalist Sir John Digby in securing Newark for the Crown.

The Royalists held Newark until 1646, during which time the defenders withstood three Parliamentarian sieges.

In February 1943, Major General Thomas Ballard and Sir John Gell had assembled a conglomerate of Parliamentarian forces from Nottingham, Lincoln and Derby outside Newark's fortifications. Henderson, however, with artillery and soldiers, repelled the Parliamentarian advances. Late the following day, Henderson launched a counter-attack against Gell, who had attempted to infiltrate the town from the south along Baldertongate. In disarray, the Parliamentarians withdrew, amid recriminations and accusations of cowardice and incompetence.

That same month, Queen Henrietta Maria of France, wife of Charles and queen consort England, Scotland and Ireland, returned from the continent with financial and materiel support for her husband's struggle. The queen – the Roman Catholic mother of future kings Charles II and James II – with a freshly raised army, moved on Nottingham via Newark.

The Midlands' Parliamentarian forces commander, Sir John Gell, recorded events at the time:

> In a short time, when upon a rumour of the Queen's forces coming towards Newark we were suddenly commanded of. Once afterwards the Queen's army faced Nottingham and had the other commanders been as forward to fight as ours, we had then put it to the fortune of a Battle, but it was otherwise resolved, and our horse went presently after to Leicester, with the Lord Grey and Colonel Cromwell upon pretence to fetch Colonel ... Regiment of foot, but neither those foot nor horse came any more to Nottingham. The Lieutenant Colonel, Captain ... and Captain ... with those forces left at Derby, besieged and took Sir Richard Hernwood [?] and his house in Staffordshire, being one of the strongest places in the county, exceeding with provision of all necessaries, and manned with such a company of obstinate papish and resolute thieves as the like were hardly to be found in the whole kingdom. In the absence of our horse from Nottingham the Queen passes by to Ashby [de la Zouch], her army assaults takes and plunders Burton [upon-Trent] carries away the commanders and soldiers prisoners, that since we redeemed Lieutenant Colonel Sanders, being confident of

> his promise to serve faithfully hereafter in this country we consented that he should be major of that Regiment of horse, for raising whereof his Excellency hath fairly granted a commission to Sir John Gell as Colonel during the Queen's stay at Ashby.
>
> Hastings laboured exceedingly to have their forces come against Derby, but all in vain, for our Regiment was now returned from Nottingham, and we were but weak before fortunately supplied with 20 barrels of powder, 300 muskets, 60 carbines and 60 case of pistols being the free gift of the honourable House of Commons, and which we shall ever gratefully acknowledge, and [because] we had been in more danger, for though we wrote to Nottingham for some foot, they having then above 2,000. With their danger past with the Queen, that would they not afford us any, which was the principal cause of the loss of Burton. For had we been able as we desired to have sent some foot thither, the town had been saved.
>
> (An extract from a contemporary document, Derbyshire County Records Office. Period spelling has been modernized.)

Parliamentarian 'Roundhead' re-enactment. (Courtesy Colonel Dudley Wall)

On 29 June 1943, the town committee and Parliamentarian Sir John Meldrum, placed Hutchinson in command of Nottingham Castle. He subsequently raised a regiment of foot and was appointed by parliament governor of both the castle and the town.

By this time, Royalist garrisons had been secured across the Midlands, leaving Nottingham isolated and vulnerable. Though the castle remained impregnable, on 18 September, Royalists occupied the town for five days, at the same time establishing a fortified position at Trent Bridge.

Parliamentarian Sir John Gell:

> Not long after our coming home the enemy took Nottingham town and possessed themselves of it, the Castle being in a manner besieged. They sent to us for relief, many of their soldiers being hid in the Town and in danger to be left, unless we presently relieved them. We sent Major Mollanus instantly and he joined with 3 Troops of horse from Leicester. With these he entered the Town, beat the enemy thence, though they were more in number than our men, killed many of the enemy, took 160 prisoners, redeemed of soldiers and divers other honest men.
>
> About 10 days after, the Committee of Nottingham sent to us again for help, in regard the enemy had fortified at the bridge [Trent Bridge], and cut of all passage to the Town on that side, our soldiers went again and after some time we beat the enemy from the bridge, which was of such importance, that the Governor of the Castle [Sir John Meldrum] professed to Major Mollanus, that unless our soldiers would stay and take the bridge, he would quit the Castle, and let the parliament do with him what they would. [Royalist forces only held Trent Bridge for about a month.]
>
> (An extract from a contemporary document, Derbyshire County Records Office. Period spelling has been modernized.)

Despite a reduction of Royalist forces in the Midlands – deployed to confront a Scottish army allied to Parliament that had crossed the border into northern England in January 1644 – Nottingham once more came under Royalist attack. Henry Hastings, ennobled in October 1643 as Lord Loughborough and given a commission of lieutenant general, occupied Nottingham with 1,000 troops in January 1644. A further 1,000 troops, including elements from the Newark garrison, besieged the town and castle, effectively cutting off Nottingham from the outside world. This latest attempt by the Crown to take Nottingham also petered out after a few days, the Castle proving, yet again, impossible to penetrate.

Later that year, the Royalist victory at the Battle of Newark was key in the re-establishment of the Crown's control in Nottinghamshire and elsewhere in the region. Parliamentarian Sir John Meldrum had laid siege to Newark with a force of 7,000 troops, but his inability to exact an expedient and decisive overthrow of the Royalist garrison, would cost him dearly.

On 21 March, a superior Royalist army, comprising the combined forces of Lord Loughborough and the German Prince Rupert of the Rhine, attacked Meldrum. Securing the bridge over the River Trent at Muskham, the Royalists enveloped Meldrum, who was forced to capitulate.

The fortunes of the opposing forces, however, continued to oscillate. Strengthened by the Newark victory, Prince Rupert struck north into Yorkshire, drawing on increasingly larger numbers of troops from the Midlands Royalist garrisons. On 2 July, on the expansive Marston Moor to the west of York, Prince Rupert suffered a major defeat at the hands of the Parliamentarian forces of the earls Leven and Manchester and Lord Fairfax. 1 battle was a watershed in the history of the Civil War in northern England, and ind the Midlands. By July, the Parliamentarians controlled most of Newark, until spring following year, which saw a resurgence of the Crown's strength in Nottinghamshire, I in October, Charles marched out of the region.

A third siege of Newark ensued in November 1645, the Scottish army of Lord Leven a the Northern English Army surrounding the town, only kept out by substantial fortifi tions erected after the second siege.

Then, in a dramatic turn of events, the battle-weary Charles made his way to the be guered Newark, surrendering to the Scottish at Southwell on 6 May 1646. Newark surr dered two days later. Parliament was victorious. Three years later, all in January 1949, defeated Charles I was indicted by the Rump House of Commons on a charge of treas tried, found guilty, sentenced and executed.

The Luddite Riots 1811

Chant no more your old rhymes about bold Robin Hood,
His feats I but little admire,
I will sing the achievements of General Ludd
Now the Hero of Nottinghamshire.

(Luddite song)

Early in the nineteenth century, the wool and cotton weaving industry experienc upheaval when workers rebelled against the introduction of significantly more effici power looms that threatened jobs and wages.

The following paragraph is copied from the Nottingham Review of Friday last:
'The appearance of things, from five to ten days ago, induced an apprehension, that the frame-breakers, or Luddites, as they are now called, were determined, by a sort of mixture of temerity and caution, to give additional vigour to their nocturnal operations, in despite of the Magistrates and all their authority. The apprehension, however, was unfounded: a cessation of arms, at least, has taken place; and we hope shortly to have to record the definitive articles of peace.

The case has been otherwise in Nottingham, for two frames were broken near Beckbarn, and one in the field-house, on Saturday evening; the latter was a lace frame of considerable value. On Saturday evening, before seven o'clock, three more lace frames were broken, one in Broad-marsh, and two in Navigation-row; and the machine of a third taken away, since which time the hand of violence has lain at rest.

The daringness of these two night's proceedings caused the Magistrates to have recourse to very prompt and determined measures; they increased the number of special constables, and seized the men at whose houses the frames had been broken, under an impression that they were either accessory to, or connived at, the outrages. It has been proved since, however, that the men were all from home at the time.

(*Oxford University and City Herald*, Saturday, 28 December 1811)

In March 1811, the Lord Lieutenant of Nottinghamshire, the Duke of Newcastle, called for the mobilization of the 2nd Dragoon Guards and five troops of the South Nottinghamshire Yeomanry: the Bunny, Holme Pierrepont, Newark, Clumber and Mansfield troops. This was in a direct response to the destruction of sixty-three frames in Arnold. In Bulwell, more frames were destroyed and one of the owners killed.

The dissatisfaction rapidly escalated into open civil strife, characterized by violence and machine-breaking. Troubles first surfaced in Nottinghamshire towards the end of 1811, spreading rapidly throughout the Midlands and the rest of the nation. It is generally accepted that the name Luddite was initially derived from a young stocking-frame knitter, Nedd Ludd, who demolished two weaving frames in anger in 1770. The etymology of the name then evolved into folklore, when it became commonly believed that the movement's name came from a mythical creature who lived in the Sherwood Forest, by the name of 'General Ned Ludd' or 'King Ludd'.

Frame - Breaking.
£.200 Reward.

WHEREAS, on Thursday Night last, about Ten o'Clock, a great Number of Men, armed with Pistols, Hammers and Clubs, entered the Dwelling-house of *George Ball*, framework-knitter, of Lenton, near Nottingham, disguised with Masks and Handkerchiefs over their Faces, and in other ways,---and after striking and abusing the said *George Ball*, they *wantonly* and *feloniously* broke and destroyed five STOCKING FRAMES, standing in the Work-shop; four of which belonged to *George Ball*, and one Frame, 40 gage, belonging to Mr. *Francis Braithwaite*, hosier, Nottingham: *all of which were working at the FULL PRICE.*

NOTICE IS HEREBY GIVEN,

THAT if any Person will give Information of the Offender or Offenders, or any one of them who entered such Dwelling-house and were concerned in such Felony, he or she shall receive a Reward of

£.200,

to be paid on Conviction, in the Proportions following, (viz.) £50 under the King's Proclamation, £25 from the Committee of the Corporation of Nottingham, and £125 from the said *Francis Braithwaite.*

WE, the under-signed Workmen of the above-named *George Ball*, do hereby certify that we were employed in working the under-mentioned Frames, on the Work and at the Prices hereinafter stated, when the Mob came to break them,—that we had never been abated in our Work, either by Mr. Braithwaite, the hosier, who employed the Frames, or by the said *George Ball*, our master; of whom we never complained, or had any Reason so to do.

QUALITY OF WORK.	PRICE.	WORKMEN.	OWNERS.
40 Gauge, Single Shape, Narrowed Two-plain,,	Maid's, 29 Shillings per Dozen,	Thomas Rew,	Mr. Braithwaite.
36 Gauge, Single Shape, Narrowed Two-plain,	Men's, 29 Shillings per Dozen,	John Jackson,	George Ball.
38 Guage. Single Shape, Narrowed Two-plain,	Maid's, 26 Shillings per Dozen,	Thomas Naylor,	George Ball.

NB. The other two Frames were worked to another Hosier, but at the Full Price.

THOMAS REW,
JOHN JACKSON,
THOMAS NAYLOR.

Nottingham, 25th January, 1812.

W. Tapson, Printer, Nottingham.

...ward poster appeal during the ...me-breaking unrest.

On Thursday, 21 November, the riots grew in size and strength, their destructive objectives now also diversifying to include millers and corn dealers. The fact that the jail was filling up with arrested Luddites made no impact on the rioters, who treated demands from the magistrates with contempt. Military means were now resorted to, but this comprised no more than thirty dragoons on foot.

That same day, the county sheriff invoked the '*posse comitatus*', the common- or statute-law authority of a law officer, to conscript any able-bodied man to assist him in keeping the peace. While despatching a 'special messenger' to Whitehall for urgent central government assistance, the sheriff called up the 1st and 2nd regiments of Local Militia. A further two troops of volunteer cavalry and a 'detachment of Queen's Bays' added to this number, and with the arrival of two troops of the 15th Light Dragoons imminent, Nottingham took on the appearance of a wartime garrison. The town 'was restored to a state of perfect tranquillity ... though the neighbourhood was threatened with more serious consequences'.

> To that account we add the following letter from Nottingham, dated Wednesday, Nov. 20:-
>
> 'I am enabled to say that the state of affairs in our neighbourhood is becoming much more tranquil; the system of frame-breaking has nearly subsided, but recourse has been had to destroying property (viz. hay-stacks) by fire, 2 of which were consumed on Monday evening last. Our town is now well supplied with military; the local militia are embodied, and to-day we have received a party of the 15th Light Dragoons by forced marches from Colchester.'
>
> On Thursday last an express arrived from the Sheriff of the county of Nottingham for the Newark troop of Yeomanry Cavalry to muster at the Red Hill, near Nottingham, with all possible speed, to assist in quelling the disturbances which have taken place in that neighbourhood. The troop mustered with that alacrity which does them the greatest credit, and arrived at the place appointed by half-past four o'clock in the afternoon, where they halted and formed into line. There appearing no disposition to riot that night, and the Bunny troop being upon the ground, they returned to Southwell until further orders, which arrived on Saturday at noon for their return home. They mustered 83 strong.
>
> (*Stamford Mercury*, Friday, 22 November 1811)

By mid-December, authorities estimated the number of rioters at 3,000, but at any on time, no more than 30 would gather to 'execute whatever mischief they have planne and disperse with great facility before the military are apprised of their movements'. Th situation, compounded by specifically tasked parties of Luddites employing terror tacti to collect money from the populace for their cause, was being described as unparalleled Nottinghamshire's history 'since the troublesome days of Charles the First, against whic misguided Monarch it took so decided a part'.

By mid-January 1812, Nottingham was reported to be in a 'state of alarm'. In one wee forty-four frames had been destroyed, the Luddite action often accompanied by dama to private property and physical violence perpetrated by gangs armed with pistols. (the evening of Sunday, 19 January, an estimated thirty to fifty men

> beset every house and avenue near their seat of action, to prevent an alarm, while a number of their companions entered a house, where, in about ten minutes, they

NOTIFICATION FROM THE MAGISTRATES OF THE COUNTY OF NOTTINGHAM TO THE TROOPS EMPLOYED IN PRESERVING THE PUBLIC PEACE OF THE COUNTY.

The Magistrates of the County of Nottingham beg to inform the Officers and Soldiers now employed in the suppression of the riots and unlawful assemblies of persons to commit felony in the County, that the troops are of themselves, and without the presence of a Magistrate, authorised and empowered to disperse, or apprehend, any of the persons meeting for the purposes above-mentioned.

Signed George Sculthorpe
Clerk to the County Magistrates.
Nottingham, Nov. 27th, 1811

demolished eight lace-frames, the holder of which, (four of them were his own) had long been in the habit of paying his workmen partly in goods.

There were three men and three women in the house, the whole of whom, with the exception of one of the latter, who was expected every moment to fall in travail, were compelled to retire into a pantry, and, with the deepest imprecations, were threatened with instant death if they dared to issue a word or a groan.

Three regiments of troops were deployed into Nottingham and the county during the month, but this did not deter the Luddites. Round the clock military patrols were instituted, giving 'the appearance of a state of warfare', but the rioters brazenly continued wreaking havoc – in one evening at Lenton, twenty frames were destroyed 'within a few hundred yards' of army barracks.

Two nights later, Luddites crossed the Trent and broke fourteen frames at Ruddington and twenty at Clifton. A troop of Hussars and elements of Bunny Troop of the Southern Nottinghamshire Cavalry were immediately mobilized. Half the force set off in pursuit, while the remainder blocked all river crossings over the Trent for a distance of four miles. Unfazed, the rebels 'seized a boat, which nobody else thought of, and repassed the river in two divisions, in perfect safety, and escaped'.

A contemporary engraving, 'The Leader of the Luddites'.

Arguably, the most audacious Luddite action that month took place at Basford, north of the Nottingham town centre:

> While three soldiers were in the house of one W. Barns, to protect three frames, a party of Luddites entered the house, and immediately confined the soldiers; and while two of the party stood sentry at the door with the soldiers' muskets, others demolished the frames; and, when the mischief was done, the muskets were discharged and the soldiers liberated, and the depredators wished them a good night.

In March, the *Bristol Mirror* reported that, since the commencement of the 'Luddite system', in Nottingham, 42 lace frames , and 544 plain silk and cotton stocking frames had been destroyed. A value of £60 was placed on each of the silk frames, and £18–£20 on the latter. With the Assizes – civil and criminal court – drawing near, there was growing anxiety among Nottingham's citizenry, not only for the safety of the county jail, but also for their town. Military guards had been placed on guard both inside and outside the jail itself, but there was growing concern that the soldiers would desert their posts as soon as the judges arrived. Mayor William Wilson had also received a letter from the Luddites, threatening to set the torch to Nottingham should any of their incarcerated comrades be found guilty and punished.

The advent of spring heralded a period of calm in Nottinghamshire, allowing for the transfer of military units to a significant increase in Luddite 'unlawful outrages' in Lancashire. The 800-strong Buckinghamshire Militia, commanded by Colonel Young moved from Mansfield to Preston, taking with them two field artillery pieces. From Nottingham itself, Lieutenant Colonel Ravenshaw's 600-strong Berkshires joined Young in Preston. An indication of the desire to restore a semblance of normality in the county was the decision to hold a militia training camp in Sherwood Forest in May, mustering 3,000 infantry and 500 cavalry from as far afield as Somerset, West Essex, Edinburgh and Surrey.

In London, Government remained concerned. In July, the House of Commons deliberated over a 'Report of the Secret Committee' into the ongoing civil unrest perpetuated by the so-called Luddites. Foreign Secretary and leader of the House, Robert Stewart, generally referred to as Lord Castlereagh, contended that His Majesty's government, hitherto satisfied with the 'alacrity' of magistrates in the affected areas to cope with the riot now faced the very real threat of having to deal with a foe that was obtaining arms and equipment, which meant that magistrates 'could no longer act without extraordinary assistance'.

> In Nottingham, the insurgents had assumed a warlike character – there oaths were administered, and organisation adopted, and atrocious crimes were committed. The House must now look upon these proceedings as a malignant combination, dangerous to the peace and security of the empire.
>
> In this situation, he should propose a remedy equal to the necessity of the case, and nothing more. He would invest the Magistrates with power to search for, and seize stolen and secreted arms. But something more was necessary to prevent tumultuous meetings, and the practice adopted of training to military duty and array.
>
> It was desirable that it [the bill] should extend equally to nocturnal meetings, and to meetings in the day time, and it would therefore be framed so as to give the Magistrates

power immediately to disperse all tumultuary meetings, whether they were for the purpose of training or drilling themselves in the use of arms or not.

(*Perthshire Courier*, Thursday, 16 July 1812)

The Frame Breaking Act criminalized machine-breaking, which carried a maximum penalty of death. In some cases in Nottingham assizes, convicted frame-breakers were sentenced to seven and fourteen years' transportation, an alternative to hanging.

With the passing of time, and unstoppable advances in mechanized weaving to replace the traditional domestic stocking frames, incidents of frame-breaking in Nottinghamshire became less and less. A core of diehard Luddites continued with civil disobedience where they could, but even these tapered off. However, it would be several years before the new wide-frames became universally adopted by hosiers across the county.

Since the civil war of the 1640s, never has England come so close to a revolution. There can be little doubt that central government's rapid flexing of military muscle in the affected areas proved to be a deciding deterrent, albeit to cries of heavy handedness in certain liberal quarters. The role of the soldier, however, was almost entirely that of endorsing the new laws granted to magistrates to address the troubles. It may also be argued that the natural fear of death at the end of a rope was the absolute deterrent – seventeen Luddites were executed, all of them in York.

Execution of the Luddites at York.

Precisely at eleven o'clock, on Saturday, the following [seven] persons suffered the sentence of the law, due to their crimes. [They] behaved in the most penitent and contrite manner we ever witnessed, placed in the melancholy situation in which they were. During the time the Ordinary was performing the functions of his duty, the repeated and earnest prayers of the culprits might be heard at a considerable distance, supplicating the Divine Being to receive their souls into everlasting rest.

John Hill addressed the populace nearly in the following terms:-

'I hope my good Christians, you will take warning by the punishment you will see this day inflicted upon me and my fellow companions. I lived for a number of years in the possession of vital religion, but unfortunately the fascinations of the world gained an ascendency over my mind, and I fell away from God and the paths of rectitude about half-a-year ago. I warn you, who now hear me, against the commission of mine, or any other crimes, which may subject you to the ignominious death I am now going to suffer.'

The bodies, after hanging till twelve o'clock, were then cut down.

(*Hampshire Chronicle*, Monday, 25 January 1813)

'The Nottingham Captain' and the Pentrich Plot 1817

In Nottingham during March 1817, sporadic and often spontaneous riots broke out, fuelled by low wages and high costs of food in the wake of the Napoleonic War. In a matter of days, elements of the Nottingham Troop quashed the unrest, but dissatisfaction, mainly among the poor continued to simmer.

One such malcontent was a 32-year-old army deserter and unemployed stocking maker, Jemiah Brandreth, a resident of the Nottinghamshire town of Sutton-in-Ashfield.

In May that year, Brandreth, himself a Luddite, met with a certain William Oliver ('Oliver the Spy') who, unbeknown to Brandreth, was a suspected agent provocateur on

It appears that two or three previous days, and at length that Monday the 9th instant was fixed for a general insurrection in Lancashire, Yorkshire, Derbyshire and Nottinghamshire, and that immense bodies of men, armed with guns, pikes and other offensive weapons, were to have marched out of Lancashire & Yorkshire, over the northeastwardly side of this county, and the westwardly side of Nottinghamshire, into the town of Nottingham.

They were to have forced into their service every person found on their march, and capable of affording them any assistance, and to have provided further supplies of arms, particularly guns, which they were most in want of, by taking them out of private houses and depots of military stores.

It seems that they were to have remained at Nottingham and to have established a provisional government there until they heard of the success of similar operations in other parts of the kingdom, and a convention was then to be held for the information of a constitution according to their own notions of civil and religious liberty.

(*Leicester Journal*, Friday, 27 June 1817)

Jeremiah Brandreth, the 'Nottingham Captain'.

the Home Office's payroll, sent by Home Secretary Lord Sidmouth to entrap Luddites. During the meeting, Brandreth was persuaded by Oliver to participate in a plot to raise an 'army' of revolutionaries numbering 50,000 to take the Tower in London and overthrow the government, bringing an 'eternal end to poverty'.

On Sunday, 8 June, Brandreth met with co-conspirators William Turner and Isaac Ludlum in the White Horse Inn in Pentrich, Derbyshire. In a packed room, Brandreth, now leader of the insurrection with the sobriquet 'the Nottingham Captain', extolled the virtues of the revolution, encouraging his captive audience to 'turn out and fight for bread'. Each volunteer would receive 100 guineas, bread, beef and ale when they joined the march to Nottingham, where they would be joined by a further 16,000 men from that county.

At 10.00 am the following morning, a rag-tag mob of 400 men, wielding a motley assortment hayforks, iron bars and sticks, assembled at Samuel Hunt's farmhouse 'in the neighbourhood of South Wingfield, in the county of Derby'.

As strong evidence that the arrival Nottingham of Brandreth's column had been anticipated, 'all due precautionary measures were tak for the effectual suppression of any local commotion, by the enrolling of special constables, and the introduction of two troops of Yeomanry Cavalry'.

At the same time, Nottingham magistrates C.G. Mundy and Lancelot Rolleston, with an escort of a detachment of 15th Hussars, commanded by Captain Phillips, set off from Nottingham to intercept the rebels. They were joined by the Holme and Newark troops of Yeomanry Cavalry and a smattering of volunteers from the former Bunny Troop. The Leicestershire Yeomanry had also been mustered and were on standby.

> It appears that the party of troops, headed by the Magistrates, came up with the advanced guard of the insurgents (consisting of about 100 men, well armed), near Gilt Brook, who after some ineffectual attempts of their leaders to induce them to stand against the troops, who were rapidly advancing, retreated and dispersed in all directions. They were as promptly pursued; many were taken with arms in their hands, ammunition, &c. and about 50 pikes, together with 20 or 30 muskets and pistols.
>
> In the town of Nottingham and its vicinity tranquillity has prevailed.
>
> (*Manchester Mercury*, Tuesday, 17 June 1817)

At 6.00 pm on the 10th, the troops returned to Nottingham, 'bringing in a waggon and cart 28 prisoners, whom they lodged in the county gaol'.

On 18 October, a Derby jury, where the conspirators had been put on trial, took only twenty minutes to find Brandreth guilty of high treason. The courtroom was 'excessively crowded, and the most profound silence prevailed while the verdict was given and recorded'. Brandreth, Turner and Ludlum were given the ultimate sentence for treason: to be hung, drawn and quartered. The Prince Regent – the future George IV – overturned the full sentence, however, reducing it to hanging and beheading.

On Friday, 7 November, Derby was awash with dragoons, militia, constables and 'javelin men', the authorities fearful of an attempt to save the men from their fate. The execution took place in the presence of a large crowd without interference, and after thirty minutes hanging, the bodies were taken down one at a time and beheaded. With no further ceremony, the three were interred in a 'deep' unmarked grave in the St Werburgh's churchyard, Derby.

The Nottingham Riot 1831

NEWS FROM THE COUNTRY

The unwelcome intelligence of the rejection of the Reform Bill by the House of Lords, arrived in Birmingham, by express, about five o'clock on Saturday afternoon. A universal feeling of disappointment and indignation pervaded the whole population; the funeral bells of the churches and chapels were immediately muffled and tolled, as upon the most solemn occasion. The Council of the Political Union assembled spontaneously in the course of the evening, and yesterday (Sunday morning), the town was placarded with the following admirable Address:-

'Address of the Council of the Birmingham Political Union, to all their fellow countrymen in the United Kingdom.

'Friends and Fellow Countrymen – The Bill of Reform is rejected by the House of Lords! Patience! Patience!! Patience!!! Our beloved King is firm. The House of Commons is firm – the whole Nation is firm. What then have the people to fear? Nothing! Unless their own violence should rashly lead to anarchy, and place difficulties in the way of the King and his Ministers. Therefore there must be no violence. The People are too strong to require violence. By Peace – by Order – everyone must rally round the Throne of the King. The small Majority of Lords will soon come to a sense of the duty which they owe to their country, and to the King, or some other legal means will be devised of carrying the Bill of Reform into a law without delay.

Fellow Countrymen – be patient – be peaceful – be strictly obedient to the laws, and every thing is yet safe.

'God bless the King.

'Thomas Attwood, Chairman.

'Saturday Evening, Oct, 8, 1831.'

The public disappointment, if not the public determination, was yesterday amply manifested in this borough, by the significant elevation of a large black flag upon the cupola of the Town-hall. The bare announcement of this sign of the times is sufficient – no comment necessary.

(*Morning Advertiser*, Monday, 10 October 1831)

Boroughs in England and Wales had since March 1831 been assiduously following the passage of the much-awaited – and longed for – Reform Bill, in anticipation of a profound overhaul of the electoral system. At the last hurdle, however, at which most believed that the required endorsement by the Tory-dominated House of Lords would be a mere formality, the peers, egged on by the anti-unionist Duke of Wellington, rejected the bill. Large-scale riots broke out across the country.

In December, the House of Commons passed the bill again, but on 7 May 1832, and in spite of a massive 200,000-strong demonstration in Birmingham, known as the Meeting of the Unions, the bill was again defeated in the Lords. Earl Grey resigned as prime minister, and William IV invited the Duke of Wellington to form a new government.

As a result of Wellington's failure to form a government, however, Grey was urgently recalled. Grey persuaded the king to create sufficient Whig peers to facilitate safe passage of the bill. Privately, and without Grey's knowledge, the monarch sternly warned the Lords that a further rejection of the bill would lead to unimaginable catastrophic consequences for Britain. The bill was passed, receiving Royal assent on 7 June 1832.

The nation edged ever closer to a violent revolution, the government's standing and reserve military resources stretched to quell nationwide riots.

That fateful Sunday, the burghers of Nottingham were 'on the tiptoe of anxiety for the London newspapers'. When the worst possible news broke in this East Midlands town, thousands took to the streets. Anger rapidly took hold, which in turn translated into violent retribution against those perceived to be in any way connected with wiping out the future political and social rehabilitation. As night fell, mobs started attacking the homes of those known to oppose the reform, all the while singing praises to their king.

At 9.00 pm, two troops of the 15th Hussars set off from the Park Barracks for the Market Place. On arrival, the large crowd feted them as the 'brave 15th', seemingly oblivious to the regiment's 'crowd control' charge in Manchester twelve years before, the so-called Peterloo Massacre in which fifteen rioters perished at the end of cavalry sabres. Assuming an extended line facing the crowd, sabres were drawn and the throng ordered

The Peterloo Massacre.

to disperse. This they did, but only to regroup elsewhere, increasingly intoxicated with the adrenalin-fuelled fervour of the mass demonstration. Provocative banners carried slogans such as 'The more those cruel tyrants bind us, the more united they will find us' and 'The Reform Bill and no Lords'.

Up to this point, a seventy-five-strong troop of the 15th Hussars was solely responsible for handling the unrest in the town itself. In spite of being rough-handled by a section of the mob, the mayor refused to call out the South Notts Yeomanry.

In July 1826, the Duke of Newcastle had been granted permission by Home Secretary and future prime minister Robert Peel to amalgamate five southern troops into a single regiment, officially titled The Southern Regiment of Nottinghamshire Yeomanry Cavalry, quickly abbreviated to South Notts Yeomanry. With a strength of 314 privates, the regiment was placed under the command of Henry Willoughby, erstwhile commander of the Wollaton Troop.

Two years later, as a direct result of the crippling costs of the war against France to the national fiscus, the South Notts was one of twenty-four regiments to be disbanded. Following civil unrest in south-west England in 1803, however, provincial yeomanry units were re-embodied, but on the basis that local landowners were required to finance the arming and equipping of the regiments which served their areas.

Fortuitously, the regiment would be required as the riots spread. On the 11th, having ridden through bad weather during the night from their respective troop centres of Watnall, Holme, Bingham and Wollaton, the outlying units assembled with the Nottingham Troop.

A 'formidable body of people' inflicted considerable damage on a mill near the race-course before arriving at Colwick Hall, the family seat of the Musters family and Lord Byron's ancestors, which the mob sacked and set ablaze.

Arming themselves with iron spikes, they tore from railings at Colwick, the crowd made the decision to attack Nottingham Castle, 'an ancient pile', and the property of the Duke of Newcastle. The ducal palace was burnt to the ground.

From the inferno at Nottingham Castle, segments of the rioters made for Beeston, where they completely razed a silk mill belonging to hosier William Lowe, before moving on to Wollaton Hall, seat of the Willoughby family and home at the time of the 6th Lord Middleton.

For the first time, however, they encountered a well-armed defence, comprising the Wollaton Troop and loyal miners. Facing them also, were a number of field pieces. As the mob surged through the gates to the hall, the yeoman charged, and after a brief skirmish, repelled the rioters, taking several of them prisoner.

Deciding to return to Nottingham where there would be softer targets, the mob unsuspectingly ran into a contingent of Yeomen and 15th Hussars, commanded by Colonel Joseph Thackwell of the 15th The South Notts. Having earlier suffered injuries at the hands of stone-throwing rioters, the troops opened fire on the mob with their pistols, wounding several. Around sixteen rioters were apprehended and carted off to the county jail. The handcuffed and their 15th Hussars escort met up with a throng in the Market Place that 'pressed closely upon the military, in a very threatening manner'.

REJECTION OF THE REFORM BILL

London, Monday, October 10.

A double guard of the first regiment of the Household Cavalry are placed at the Horse Guards, and a horse patrol is parading St, James's Park. A party of the same regiment is lying at the gun house, near the long gun in St. James's Park.

An extra guard, under the command of Captain Clayton, is ordered to the magazine in Hyde Park this morning.

Orders were also sent to Woolwich to have the artillery in readiness, should occasion require their presence in the metropolis. The troops in Hounslow Barracks are also in a state for immediate service.

Large quantities of ammunition were delivered out to the troops this morning at their respective barracks and quarters, and even the recruits at the Recruit house are under arms.

The whole of the police force stationed in the environs this morning marched into the metropolis, and are lying, some in the barracks at the King's Mews, and others in Palace-yard.

A double guard of the Scotch Fusileers or 3d Regiment of Foot Guards, consisting of 100 men, under the command of Captain Bowden and Lieutenant Rowley, are stationed in the guard-room at the Horse Guards.

(*Dublin Evening Post*, Thursday, 13 October 1831)

One of the cannon used to defend Wollaton Hall from the rioters. (Photo Gerry van Tonder)

The soldiers drew their sabres and presented their pistols. At around 5.00 pm, turning into Bridlesmith Gate from The Poultry, the escort found itself being stoned by several of the rioters in the crowd closing in on the rear of the party. This prompted an officer to randomly discharge his pistol down High Street, striking an innocent bystander, former soldier and Waterloo veteran Thomas Auckland through the chest and hitting a certain Joshua Arnold in the forehead. Ironically, at the time Auckland had been acting as a special constable.

The retort from the officer's pistol galvanized others in the escort who, sabres drawn, set about the mob, 'galloping along the foot pavements, and striking with the flat of the sword those who did not move onward'. This action was immediately followed by barricading routes into the Market Place to ensure the crowd stayed away. Shops and inns were ordered to close, while aggressive horseback patrolling of the streets by the troops continued until 9.00 pm, which 'caused the crowds to be completely dispersed ... very few persons were to be seen in or near the Market-place'.

The different troops of the South Nottinghamshire yeomanry cavalry, were stationed in the vicinity of the town [Nottingham], and small parties of them aided the military. A detachment of them proceeding up Derby-road, were assailed by a shower of stones from Chimley's close, which was returned by a smart fire; however no one was hurt, as the mob took refuge behind the wall, and then they speedily dispersed.

About eleven o'clock, large crowds of people began to assemble on the Leenside, and in the neighbourhood of the canal, but by the use of vigorous measures, they were dispersed without any mischief being done.

WEDNESDAY

The alarm appeared to have subsided in a great measure, the market was supplied as usual with cattle, vegetables, fruit, &c., and all the shops were re-opened; rumours were afloat of various attacks to be made by the mob, but they never re-assembled in any numbers; at night the smaller thorough fares into the Market-place were again closed. The patroles were on duty till about eleven o'clock, when, all being quiet, the greater part of them repaired to their respective homes.

The Magistrates have been indefatigable in their exertions to secure the peace and restore the tranquillity of the town, and we are happy in now announcing that they have succeeded.

The greatest praise is due to the Fifteenth Hussars, for the temper with which they have conducted themselves during the most trying period; constantly on duty for three nights and two days, they have uniformly behaved with firmness and moderation; and even when exceedingly provoked, did not allow themselves to be irritated.

(*Nottingham Review and General Advertiser for the Midland Counties,*
Friday, 14 October 1831)

The South Notts, with a strength of 21 officers and 274 troops, remained on indefinite duty for six days, as relative calm returned to the county. There can be no doubt that their support was instrumental in the successful and expedient putting down of the insurrection.

Wollaton Hall. (Photo Gerry van Tonder)

3. CALL TO ARMS: FOREIGN

Peninsular War, Siege of Badajoz, April 1812

From the peculiar situation of the place, it was necessary to scale, although a large breach was affected; the enemy threw down the ladders as fast as they were reared, and thus precipitated whole companies into the fosse.

When at last our men established themselves on the walls and leaped down, they fell on *chevaux de frize*, formed of old swords ground to the utmost sharpness. There were trenches and breast-works across the streets, and these also undermined ready for blowing up.

The resistance was such as men would make who fought for their last stake. The streets of Badajoz were almost excavated, and the soldier walked upon mines – every thing above ground and every thing below was in confusion – the air was rent with discharges of guns, and the explosions of shells, and the ground, by the operations of the enemy, shook, as though agitated by an earthquake.

(*Cheltenham Chronicle*, Thursday, 7 May 1812)

The Peninsular War of 1807–1814, a conflict between the allied armies of Britain, Spain and Portugal on the one hand, and the French on the other, was a campaign to oust Napoleon's forces from the Iberian Peninsula.

Having taken the Portuguese–Spanish border towns of Almeida and Ciudad Rodrigo, Sir Arthur Wellesley, the First Duke of Wellington, moved south to the strategic Spanish frontier town of Badajoz. With a strength of 27,000 troops and 52 artillery pieces, the combined British–Portuguese force arrived on 16 March 1812, and immediately went about preparing the investment of the extremely well defended French garrison of 5,000 troops under Général de Brigade Armand Philippon.

On 6 April, in one of the bloodiest battles of the Napoleonic Wars, the fortress was taken, but at considerable cost, the allied forces sustaining 4,800 casualties in a few short hours of bitter clashes (see map in the colour section).

The 45th (1st Nottinghamshire) Foot – originally formed in 1741 as the 56th Houghton's Regiment of Foot – formed part of Wellesley's 10,000-strong expedition that sailed from Cork, Ireland, on 12 July 1808, destination Mondego Bay, ninety miles north of Lisbon. Commanded by Lieutenant Colonel William Guard, the 45th's embarkation strength stood at 35 officers, 38 sergeants, 37 corporals, 22 drummers and 635 privates.

At this point, Britain ordered a further three brigades already stationed in Europe and Sir John Moore's army in the Baltic to immediately move to Portugal to join up with Wellesley. The 45th combined with the 50th and 91st to form the 5th Brigade, commanded by Brigadier General Catlin Craufurd.

At Roliça, Wellesley, with 13,700 infantry and 650 cavalry, encountered the first French outpost. Due to the broken nature of the high ground on which the Portuguese village stood, the 45th and light companies were tasked with driving the French from their ground, in what was the first engagement of the Peninsular War. This was achieved, but there were more than 1,000 casualties on both sides. Ten men of the 45th were wounded, and Ensign Dawson killed while carrying the King's colours, the staff he was carrying cut in two by cannon shot.

As the British armies slowly rolled back the French, in June 1809 Wellesley crossed into Spain at the head of 21,000 men. At this stage, the armies were reorganized, and the 45th joined up with the 24th and 31st regiments of the 3rd Division under the command of Major General John Mackenzie. The general would be killed in action at Talavera.

The heights at Talavera, seventy-five miles south-west of the Spanish capital, Madrid, proved to be an even costlier experience for the 45th, suffering 193 casualties, including Lieutenant Colonel Guard who was severely wounded.

In January 1812, Wellesley – since the victory at Talavera elevated to the peerage as Viscount Wellington – took the important city of Ciudad Rodrigo with his Anglo-Portuguese army after a two-week siege.

The 45th continued to fight in the front line, Wellington regularly mentioning the regiment in his despatches. Ciudad Rodrigo was no exception, where elements of the 45th captured one of the two cannons which, positioned in the walls, had decimated the ranks of the soldiers storming the fortifications.

British casualties were again heavy, the army losing a further two generals: Henry MacKinnon and Robert Craufurd. The 45th suffered forty-eight casualties, including the highly regarded and popular Captain Robert Hardiman. A friend of his in the 88th wrote of him and of Lieutenant William Pearse, who fell by his side during the storming of the breach:

Wellington's forces encounter the French at Roliça. (Painting by William Heath)

At length I reached the grand breach; it was covered with many officers and soldiers. Of the former, amongst others, was my old friend Hardiman of the 45th, and William Pearse of the same regiment. The once cheerful, gay Bob Hardiman lay on his back, half his head was carried away by one of those discharges of grape from the flank guns at the breach which were so destructive to us in our advance. His face was perfect, and even in death presented its wanton cheerfulness. Poor fellow! He died without pain, and regretted by all who knew him. Up to the moment of the assault he was the same pleasant Bob Hardiman who delighted every one by his anecdotes, and none more than my old corps, although many of his jokes were at our expense.

When we were within a short distance of the breach, as we met he stopped for an instant to shake hands.

'What's that you have on your shoulder?' said he, as he spied a canteen of rum which I carried.

'A little rum, Bob,' said I.

'Well,' he replied, 'I'll change my breath; and take my word for it, in less than five minutes some of the subs. will be scratching a captain's ... for there will be wigs on the green.'

He took a mouthful of rum, and taking me by the hand, squeezed it affectionately, and in ten minutes afterwards he was a corpse.

The appearance of Pearse was quite different from his companion. Ten or a dozen grape shot pierced his heart, and he lay, or rather sat, beside his friend like one asleep.

(Philip Hugh Dalbiac, *History of the 45th First Nottinghamshire Regiment, Sherwood Foresters*, Swan Sonnenschein & Co. Ltd., 1902)

On 16 March, the 'Fighting Third' 3rd Division, which held the 45th, together with the 4th and Light divisions and a brigade of Portuguese troops, arrived at the strongly fortified Badajoz, situated on the east bank of a bend in the Guadiana River.

A stronghold, the 'Picurina', had been set up by the French defenders on high ground to the east of the town. In between, a small stream had been dammed, forming a 'considerable inundation'. To the south-west of the town, was another raised defence work, the 'Pardaleras', which was connected to the main garrison by a covered passage. The castle itself was also situated on elevated ground, while farther south was the 'formidable bastion' of San Vincente.

The garrison had a strength of 5,000, compared to Wellington's 27,000, but the French commander, Général de Brigade Armand Philippon, was a strong leader 'almost unequalled for his energy, steadfastness, and fertility of resource'.

On the night of the 17th, work began on the digging of trenches parallel to and only 160yd from Picurina. After a delay caused by heavy rains flooding some of the trenches, the 5th Division took up a siege position on the right bank of the river. On the 25th, batteries of artillery were positioned along the 600yd length of the trench, which had a 4,000yd communications trench leading up to it. The guns included ten 24-pounders, eleven 18-pounders and seven 5 ¼" howitzers, all of which opened fire on the following day.

After this softening-up barrage, accompanied by intimidatory rifle fire from British marksmen, Major General Sir James Kempt, by this time in command of the 3rd Division, received orders to assault the Picurina garrison.

Peninsular War
French cuirassier and
infantry re-enactment.
(Courtesy Myrabella)

At 9.00 pm, Kempt assembled 500 of his men and, keeping 100 in reserve in the trenches, he sent out two flanking columns of 200 each, skirting the French position to the left and right. Headed by engineers equipped with ladders and axes, the two columns simultaneously stormed the palisades. Despite a withering curtain of fire, the troops scrambled over the palisades and up to the ramparts, where vicious close-quarter fighting ensued. Having lost almost all of his officers, and half the garrison wiped out by the assailants, the French commander Gaspar Thiery surrendered. Kempt, securing the position with three battalions, immediately set about digging a second parallel trench.

The breaching guns commenced a bombardment on 30 March, and by 6 April, three breaches had been created in the castle and ancillary defences' walls – the right flank and curtain of La Trinidad bastion, and the left flank of Santa Maria.

All four divisions were employed in the assault. The Light Division attacked the main breach, while the 5th Division made a feint at Pardaleras before striking at San Vincente. The 4th Division was tasked with the smaller breaches at La Trinidad and Santa Maria, leaving the 'Fighting Third' to escalade the castle. The H-hour was set for 10.00 pm that night.

Before the appointed time for the attack, however, a carcass – incendiary shell – fired from the castle revealed the position of the 3rd Division, immediately drawing fire on the waiting troops. Knowing it was pointless to tarry, Kempt, in the absence of Lieutenant General Thomas Picton who was yet to arrive at the staging point, led the 'Fighting Third' on the attack.

The troops, headed by their ladder men lugging the largest ladders available, crossed the bridge over the Rivillas in single file, taking heavy fire from the castle. As the advanced over the broken terrain towards the foot of the castle walls, Kempt fell, severely wounded. As he was evacuated to the rear, Picton and his staff arrived.

In the advance, Kempt's brigade formed the right of the column, while Colon Campbell with the 5th, 77th, 83rd and 94th regiments took the left. With light companies from all the regiments providing an advance guard, the 45th (1st Nottinghamshire Regiment led the whole column from the centre.

The exposed and bunched-up 3rd Division suffered considerable losses from French light-ball fire. The ladders, which proved too short, were pushed away as soon as they were raised against the castle walls. At the same time, 'stones, logs of wood, and all sorts of missiles made terrible havoc among the men'.

Eventually, and against all odds, three ladders were secured. Lieutenant James Macpherson of the 45th was the first to clamber up, only to find his ladder was 3ft short of the rampart. Unconcerned, Macpherson called on the men below him to heave him up, but in the process, he was shot, falling 'insensible' into a ditch below and breaking two ribs.

In spite of the growing pile of dead and wounded at the base of the castle walls, the troops persevered and started to gain the upper hand as they scaled the parapets and dropped into the castle itself. Reports stated

British grenadiers and fusiliers, Napoleonic Wars. (Courtesy Richard Knötel)

that Corporal Kelly of the 45th was the first to spring down into the castle. Desperate hand-to-hand combat ensued as the 3rd pushed the French through the castle gates and into the town.

General Picton was also wounded, sustaining a shot in the groin, but after twenty-five minutes, 'rose up and cheered his men on to the attack'. Picton would be killed in action while leading a bayonet charge at Waterloo on 18 June 1815.

Macpherson, although wounded, bleeding and in considerable pain, also recovered, and once more scaled a ladder into the castle. He immediately made his way to the keep where the French Tricolore was flying. Disposing of a sentry in his way, Macpherson reached the flagstaff and hauled down the enemy's flag. He then hoisted his own scarlet jacket, attesting to the gallant part the 45th had performed in the attack.

To commemorate the victory of the 45th, every year on 6 April, the anniversary of the regiment's heroic assault on Badajoz castle in 1812, a scarlet jacket is raised on a flagstaff at the 2nd Battalion Mercian Regiment's (Worcesters and Foresters) Nottinghamshire headquarters at Foresters House in Chilwell.

Elsewhere, the assault met with little success, and with the casualties now in excess of 5,000, Wellington ordered his troops to retire to regroup. His instructions to Picton, fully grasping the strategic imperative of their position, was to hold the castle at all costs.

Shortly thereafter, the 5th Division, attacking the breach for the second time, poured into the town. The British troops had now gained entry in three places, and with the castle refuge also lost, General Philippon surrendered his garrison.

What followed was described at the time as a scene of 'riot and debauch unequalled in the annals of the British army; the chains of discipline were thrown off, and the whole force gave themselves up to pillage, intoxication, and wanton destruction to life and property'.

Second Anglo-Afghan War, 1878–1880

We now enter upon the story of a more noble and stirring strife ... a strife in which hard battles were brilliantly fought with fierce and hardy enemies, and in most instances won; in which a hard march was made by Roberts and his gallant column second to none in the annals of war, and in which a rich reward of glory and Victoria Crosses was gathered.

(James Grant, *British Battles on Land and Sea*, Cassell and Co. Ltd., London, 1899)

The nineteenth century witnessed considerable diplomatic posturing between Britain and Russia, as they vied for the expansion and retention of Asia in their respective spheres of influence.

In 1837, British Foreign Secretary, Lord Palmerston, expressed concern that both internal political instability in Afghanistan and the growing might of the Sikhs to the northwest, increased the possibility of a Russian invasion of British India via Afghanistan. The British East India Company had despatched an envoy to Kabul with the express objective of forming an alliance with the Afghanistan Amir Dost Mohammad Khan against Russia. Having recently lost Peshawar to the Sikh Punjab empire, the amir indicated a willingness to side with Britain, but on condition that they assist him to retake Peshawar.

For the British, however, this did not even warrant consideration, for the simple reason that the Sikh army, the *Dal Khalsa*, would present a far more formidable foe than the amorphous tribal jihadists who would fight for their amir only when called upon to do so. Regarded as one of the strongest forces on the sub-continent, the huge Sikh army, bound by an all-pervasive faith, had been trained by French officers and were equipped with modern arms. For the British, therefore, an alliance with the Maharajah of the Punjab Ranjit Singh, would be preferable.

Sher Ali, Amir of Kabul. (Source *Recent British Battles*)

Dost Mohammad's attempt to attract the British by appointing Russian Ambassador Yan Vitkevich failed when negotiations with Moscow broke down. The Russian then switched their support to the Iranian Qajar dynasty in Persia, a move seen by Britain as confrontational, and a strategy by Tsar Nicholas to undermine British control in India. When, in late 1837, Qajar forces crossed into Afghanistan and laid siege to the city of Herat, British India acted.

Governor General of India, George Eden, 1st Earl of Auckland, felt the time had arrived to re-install deposed Shuja Shah on the Afghan throne. In December, 21,000 British, Sikh and Indian troops set off from the Punjab for Kabul.

By 1842, comprehensively beaten by the terrain, weather and the Afghan style of engagement, what was left of the expedition returned to India via the Khyber Pass, allowing Dost Mohammad to resume his seat in Kabul.

In 1878, the perceived Russian threat forced the British to launch a second expedition into Afghanistan to remove the incumbent ruler and son of Dost Mohammad, Sher Ali Khan – but, having learned costly lessons from the first war, planning was thorough and detailed. Three columns would simultaneously invade Afghanistan along the three main arterial routes into the country. To the north, Lieutenant General Samuel Browne would lead the Peshawar Field Force in clearing the Khyber and the valleys beyond of Afghan forces. Just to the south, Major General Frederick Roberts VC, commanding the Kurram Valley Field Force – the smallest of the three columns – would clear a series of passes through the Kurram, thereby opening a secure route to the Afghan capital, Kabul. The third column, the Kandahar Field Force, under Lieutenant General Sir Donald Stewart, would infiltrate farther south, where he faced the most difficult task of the three British forces. Stewart would have to push through the unforgiving Bolan Pass in the Central Makran Range and the Kojuk Pass to secure the Pashtun city of Kandahar.

The overall expedition strategy was to replace the existing amir and then to withdraw to India via the Khyber. Leading up to this, Stewart would secure and place Kandahar in the hands of a Bombay division drawn from his force, as part of a plan to establish a British-controlled state of Kandahar, separate from the rest of Afghanistan. He would

eneral Sir Donald Stewart.
ource *Recent British Battles*)

then march the rest of his force to Roberts at Kabul, from where the expedition would withdraw, mission accomplished.

Stewart's 7,200-strong force of British and Indian troops was made up of two divisions:

THE 1ST DIVISION, commanded by Lieutenant General Stewart:

Cavalry Brigade under Brigadier General Walter Fane – 15th Hussars, 8th Cavalry and 19th Fane's Lancers;

Royal Artillery under Brigadier General C. G. Arbuthnot – one horse battery, three field batteries, two heavy batteries, three siege batteries and one mountain battery;

First Infantry Brigade under Brigadier General R. Barter – 2nd Battalion King's Royal Rifles, 15th Sikhs and 25th Punjabis;

Second Infantry Brigade under Brigadier General W. Hughes – 59th (2nd Nottinghamshire) Regiment, 12th Kelat-i-Ghilzai Regiment, 1st Gurkhas and 3rd Gurkhas.

THE 2ND DIVISION, commanded by Major General M. A. Biddulph.

Cavalry Brigade under Brigadier General C. H. Palliser – 21st Daly's Horse, 22nd Sam Browne's Horse and 35th Scinde Horse;

Artillery under Colonel le Mesurier – one field battery and two mountain batteries;

First Infantry under Brigadier General R. Lacy – 70th East Surrey, 19th Punjabis and 127th Baluchis;

Second Infantry Brigade under Brigadier General Nuttall – 26th Punjabis, 32nd Pioneers, 55th Coke's Rifles and 129th Baluchis.

Dominated by native Indian regiments from the Bengal, Bombay and Madras armies, the British relied heavily on the so-called 'martial races' – Baluchis, Gurkhas, Sikhs, Jats, Pathans, and Muslim and Hindu Punjabis. Armed with .45 Martini-Henri rifles, the British had now largely adopted khaki uniforms for use in the field.

On 4 January 1879, on the 'sandy wastes' of the approach to the Kandahar plain, Brigadier Palliser, with an advanced guard of cavalry, encountered the enemy at Saifuddin, where two roads pass through a series of gorges no more than 400yd apart. Engagements involved sporadic and brief skirmishes, the British forces employing sword and cannon to send their assailants back towards Kandahar.

On the morning of the 6th, Stewart's two divisions converged at Muhammed Amin, now only a few days' march from Kandahar. At this point, after having expected to easily procure food for the column, the commissariat was no longer able to feed the troops. In spite of the area through which Stewart marched being 'peopled and richly cultivated', the Afghan jihadis had plundered everything they could lay their hands on. When the column came across villages with food, it was expected of each individual soldier to source his own sustenance. Unfortunately, however, the local populace was allowed to freely and openly sell to the highest bidder, something which a correspondent referred to as 'the outrageous proceedings of the Afghans. Unluckily no prices are laid down, nor any system of obtaining supplies'.

On the 15th, Stewart halted his column at Khusab, fifteen miles from his objective. Intelligence had been received that 'only 4,000 horse and one regiment of infantry' garrisoned Kandahar, armed with smooth-bore muskets. At noon the following day, Stewart took Kandahar without firing a shot, the amir's troops having fled to Kabul.

Stewart immediately set about establishing on authoritative administration in Kandahar. The 59th, after having lost only two soldiers in action in February – privates J. Friend and J. Wardall – lost a further twenty-eight through disease during the regiment's interlude in the city. Yet again, further evidence of fatal stomach ailments and tropical diseases that plagued Victoria's troops in campaigns on foreign soil.

To the north, however, Roberts lost Kabul. Having restored Amir Yakoub Kahn to his throne in the capital – an extremely unpopular event with the regional tribal clans – Roberts moved his troops and his headquarters into the fortified Sherpur cantonment just to the north of Kabul. Tens of thousands of heavily armed tribesmen under fanatic Mohammed Jan, immediately filled the void created by the departure of the British from the city.

> The people of Cabul now freely sympathised with the tribal bands who occupied it, thereby forfeiting their claim to the clemency of General Roberts; and every quarter of it was now invested by disbanded vagabonds of the Ameer's late army, deserters from the provincial forces, refugees from justice in India and Persia, armed swashbucklers of the genuine Oriental type, steeped to the lips in cruelty and crime, and only waiting fresh opportunities for pillage and slaughter.
>
> Thus December [1879] saw the whole country once more aflame. A *jehad* or holy war was preached; the Governor of Maidan, whom we had appointed, was murdered, and the army of General Roberts was seriously menaced and imperilled by an extensive rising of the warlike tribes.
>
> (James Grant, *British Battles on Land and Sea*, Cassell and Co. Ltd., London, 1899)

Just before Christmas, Roberts, having survived sustained Afghan assaults on Sherpur, broke out of Sherpur to ruthlessly deal with armed stragglers of the fleeing tribesmen. He then turned his attention to the critical task of restoring control of Kabul. Mohammed Jan, with his enormous following, however, had managed to evade the British, making for the city of Ghazni on the road to Kandahar.

By February, Roberts received intelligence of a renewed mustering of tribal forces in Ghazni province, which had become the Afghanistan stronghold of Mohammed Jan and the mullah Mushki-i-Alam, both of who were responsible for the attacks on Roberts's headquarters in Sherpur. Believing that Kabul would again receive the attentions of those wishing to oust the British from Kabul, preparations were made to neutralize the growing threat, including the employment of Stewart's Kandahar Field Force to take Ghazni on its march towards Kabul. A column from the capital would simultaneously march south for a prearranged rendezvous with Stewart at Sheikhabad.

On 27 March 1880, with a column of only 7,000 troops and as many camp followers, Stewart left Kandahar, initially dividing his force into two, one on each side of the Tarnak River. Stewart called a two-day halt on 6 April, by now fully cognizant of a substantial force of Hazara tribesmen shadowing their progress. At Jan Murad, and now well into the Ghazni province, the two columns met. On the 18th, the consolidated army marched towards Ghazni, some twenty-five miles distant (see map in colour section).

The following morning, at first light, the enemy was sighted in what was described as a good position near Ahmed Khel in the Galkoh mountains. Beyond this point, the open terrain would not suit Afghan tactics. Estimated at 15,000 mounted and foot tribesmen, the enemy position extended across Stewart's front and along his left flank. His column was

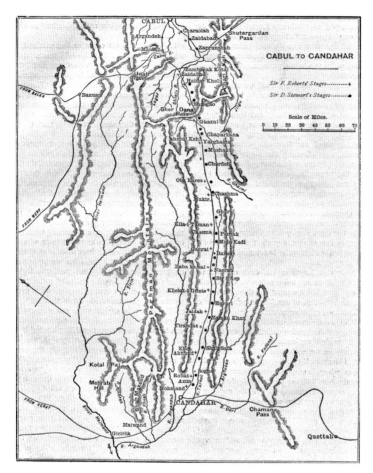

CABUL TO CANDAHAR

Sir F. Roberts' Stages ....+

Sir D. Stewart's Stages .... •

The route between Kabul and Kandahar. (Source *Recent British Battles*)

strung out over six miles, the 19th Bengal Lancers and the 19th Punjabi Native Infantry (PNI) making up the advance guard, with Palliser and six guns of the Royal Horse Artillery in support. Stewart and his command came next, followed by Hughes and his 2nd Infantry Brigade that included the 59th and three Indian regiments. The transport column, escorted by Barter's 1st Infantry Brigade, brought up the rear.

On drawing near to the enemy positions

> the infantry brigade of General Hughes was ordered to 'form for attack;' the markers hurried to the front; the brigade was ordered to lie down while the artillery, under Walters and Campbell, moved forward and opened fire at 1,200 yards range, or at 1,500 yards, according to another account; but so rapid was the advance of the foe, that the range had to be quickly reduced to 400, and finally to case-shot distance. The latter was soon expended, and then the guns were loaded with shrapnel, with heads towards the charge, to explode at the muzzle, a process that covered the ground before the cannon with heaps of dying and dead, fearfully torn and mutilated.
>
> (James Grant, *British Battles on Land and Sea*, Cassell and Co. Ltd., London, 1899)

Roberts's Sikh orderlies.
(Source *Recent British Battles*)

Farther down on the column's left flank, mounted Afghan tribesmen swept over the hill, sweeping down on the line of infantry before it was even able to advance. Such was the momentum of the 'fanatic and frantic' enemy cavalry, 'their bright tulwars and charahs flashing in the sun, with streaming banners and wild yells', that they rolled back the 19th Bengal Lancers into the 3rd Gurkhas, causing a great deal of confusion as the infantry momentarily lost its cohesion. The mêlée spilled into the 59th to the right of the Gurkhas, backfooting the Nottinghamshires who, without bayonets fixed, were still in the process of wheeling in formation to face the screaming Afghans bearing down on them.

For a few desperate moments, in the seemingly directionless milling around of the British in the noise and dust, and stunned by the strength of the Afghan mounted assault, it appeared that Stewart was facing defeat. Having come down the hill in two ravines in the shape of a V, the enemy's right cavalry, under concealment of a grassy ridge, was moving to turn Stewart's left flank. Stewart, personally directing the battle on the ground, where on two occasions Ghazni tribesmen almost hacked their way to him, immediately strengthened his left with a squadron of the 19th Lancers.

General Ross's division crosses the Logar River to meet General Stewart. (Source *Recent British Battles*)

Despite the initial disarray, compounded by the unprepared 59th, the centre infantry 'assumed the shape of a semi-circle, with a gap in the centre'. The soldiers stood firm bringing to bear 'a terrific fire into their line, while the artillery ploughed them down with showers of grape; and the cavalry, with lances levelled, made several splendid charges through their dense and yelling masses'.

Stewart, wishing to capitalize on a slow turning of the battle in his favour, threw his whole reserve into the fight, in support of both the infantry and the artillery.

To the left of the infantry, the 3rd Gurkhas again came under threat from the Ghazni horse. Pre-empting a potential overwhelming of their position, Colonel Gyster immediately formed his Gurkhas into company squares, each separated by a gap so that 'friend and foes could pass together'.

As the mounted Ghazni swept through these spaces, the Gurkhas opened up on them with a 'blighting fire of musketry', to which the Nottinghamshires, the 2nd Sikhs and the 19th Punjabis contributed.

Most fearful was the effect of this sudden and concentrated fire. In the wildest confusion, rising, sinking, kicking, plunging, and rolling over each other, went the Afghan cavalry; and then our own, relieved from the pressure on their rear, fell upon the shattered column [of Afghans] with lance and sword, hurling it back through or between the squares, and the great crisis of the day was over.

The whole enemy fell back, and though a body of them, under cover of some villages and orchard walls, kept up a parting fire, which hit a few, they all fled ultimately; Colonel Maclean, with the 1st Punjab Cavalry, dashed off in hot pursuit, and falling upon a body that had rallied on an eminence, he hewed them down on all sides, and once again the headlong flight was resumed.

(James Grant, *British Battles on Land and Sea*, Cassell and Co. Ltd., London, 1899)

For Stewart, the victory was complete and crushing.

'A blow has been inflicted upon the Afghans,' said a correspondent at the time, 'from which they will be long ere they recover.'

Stewart suffered seventeen killed and 115 wounded. The 59th's Private J. Cunningham was killed in action, while Private J. Wood succumbed to his wounds the next day. Commanding Officer Lieutenant Colonel Lawson and Lieutenant Watson were the only wounded officers from the regiment. More than 1,000 Afghan fighters lay dead, and it was estimated that a further 2,000 were wounded.

Stewart immediately regrouped his men and marched to Nani, just nine miles from Ghazni, from where he sent elements of his cavalry to reconnoitre the city. They found, however, that the warring Ghilzies had fled, with their leader, Mohammed Jan. In a repeat of the Kandahar experience, Stewart rode into Ghazni without having to fire a shot.

On 25 April, Stewart marched from Ghazni, arriving in Kabul on 2 May, where he took command, with 'the general control of political affairs'. On 12 August, Stewart assembled his forces and started the arduous and hazardous march back to India.

First World War, Gommecourt, The Somme, 1 July 1916

[I] put my head over the parapet – for all was dull and quiet – and stared at the silent and thorny German lines. But in spite of appearances the Germans (who held a sharp salient in Gommecourt Wood) were known to be forewarned and forearmed. At 7.30 a.m., and earlier on July 1st their guns – closely concentrated and of full calibre – set up a triple barrage (fire curtain).

Through all these three barrages of intense fire our men marched quite steadily, as if nothing was in the way, as if they were under review. At every step men fell; and our trenches are very far apart from the German. The gap was still wide, though a little while before the fighting we had built a completely new trench nearer the enemy, in the course of a single night.

When these steady, steadfast soldiers, true to death, paraded in more than decimated numbers through and across the third barrage, the enemy – in their turn heroic – left their trenches, erected machine guns on the parapets, and fought one another in the open.

I have not the hardihood to write more. Heroism could no further go.

Our men died, and dying held in front of them enough German guns to have altered the fate of our principal and our most successful advance in the south.

They died defeated, but won as great a victory in spirit, and in fact, as English History or any other history will ever chronicle.

(War Correspondent Sir William Beach Thomas writing from The Somme on the British assault on Gommecourt, 1 July 1916)

Sherwood Foresters bomb-carrying party. (Photo Ernest Brooks)

Established in 1881 and retitled in 1902, The Sherwood Foresters (Nottinghamshire and Derbyshire Regiment) was a line infantry regiment of the British army. The 7th Battalion, commonly referred to as the Robin Hoods as it is most closely associated with Nottingham, replaced the Robin Hood Rifles on the formation of the Territorial Army in 1908.

In July 1914, the Robin Hoods were in camp at Hunmanby, Yorkshire, with the Notts and Derby Brigade, at a time when the tense situation in Western Europe was a common topic of conversation and speculation.

On the 31st, Tsar Nicholas II mobilized his Russian forces, precipitating a declaration of *kriegsgefahrzustand* – conditions of danger of war – from Germany's Kaiser Wilhelm II, and a demand to Russia to demobilize within twelve hours. Giving France a similar ultimatum, Wilhelm required a declaration from President Raymond Poincaré that, in the event of war with Russia, he would remain neutral. France would, however, honour its treaty of alliance with Russia.

Three days later, orders were received for the camp to be struck, and for all battalions to return to base and await further instructions. Late at night that same day, 3 August, the Robin Hoods arrived at Nottingham's Victoria Station, where townsfolk 'turned out in numbers to meet her Regiment, and the reception "The Robin Hoods" received, though by no means demonstrative, was full of deep and significant cordiality'.

Later that same evening, Britain issued a declaration of war on Germany, after the Kaiser failed to formally state that Germany would respect the neutrality of Belgium. Britain immediately called up its army reserves and mobilized territorial forces.

The Commanding Officer of the 1/7th Battalion, the Robin Hoods, upon receiving his instructions by telegram on 4 August, wired all his officers and despatched embodiment notices to all other ranks. Public notices for the call to the colours were posted throughout the city, giving the headquarters on Derby Road as the mustering point. At 9.00 am, the following day, the battalion paraded in full marching order. The roll call revealed only seven absentees, but they arrived later that day.

Lunch for Foresters on the Ancre. (Photo John Warwick Brooke)

It was a day when all felt proud to be Englishmen: a wonderful dignity clothed the whole nation and an almost religious seriousness appeared upon the surface current of its daily life. At last the territorials were to be put to the test.

For the past fifty years as Volunteers or Territorials they had been considered by many to be 'playing at soldiers', and were often the object of ill-timed jest; surely no one again will ever doubt the value of the Citizen Soldiers; in many a hard fight they have more than justified themselves.

(Lieutenant Colonel Arthur W. Brewill, Commanding Officer,
1/7th (Robin Hood) Battalion, Sherwood Foresters)

ntensive training and route marching ensued, including at Derby, where the Robin Hoods joined up with the 1/5th of Derby, both now battalions of the 139th (Sherwood Foresters) Brigade. Commanded by Brigadier General C.T. Shipley CB, the brigade also included 1/6th and 1/8th battalions, Sherwood Foresters, in addition to 1/4th Battalion the Black Watch, 1/3rd (City of London) Battalion, London Regiment (Royal Fusiliers), 139th Machine Gun Company and 139th Mortar Battery.

The 139th travelled to Luton, the designated concentration point for the 46th (North Midland) Division, where they joined up with the 137th (Staffordshire) and 138th (Lincoln and Leicester) brigades. Commanded by Major General the Honourable E.J. Montagu-Stuart-Wortley CB, CMG, DSO, the division also carried the usual mounted troops, brigades of artillery, companies of engineers, transport and machine guns, field ambulances and a mobile veterinary section.

On 21 August, the brigade was moved to Harpenden for further training, medical examination and immunization against enteric fever. At a parade on 14 October, the brigade was inspected first by their divisional commander and then by Field Marshal Lord

Roberts VC. During October, companies of the Robin Hoods attended intensive musketry courses and range practice at Warden Hill.

The battalion saw the year out in Luton once more, having been moved around a fair amount, during which training was non-stop. Here the troops were issued with 'M.L.E. Mark I Charger Loader re-sighted for Mark VII ammunition'.

Finally, and having earlier been inspected by the King at Hallingbury Park, the Robin Hoods sailed from Southampton for France, assembling at Le Havre on 28 February 1915.

Typically, the Robin Hoods were moved often – Kemmel, Locra, Ploegsteert, Hohenzollern Redoubt. At the latter, Captain Charles Geoffrey Vickers would earn the Victoria Cross. By late January 1916, the men from Nottingham found themselves at Vimy Ridge on the Hindenburg Line, just north of the French town of Arras and above the northern stretch of the Somme at Gommecourt.

At the end of 1915, General Sir Douglas Haig took over as commander-in-chief of the British Expeditionary Force (BEF) on the Western Front. He immediately set about exploring the possibilities of a large British spring offensive. By February, Haig had ordered General Sir Henry Rawlinson, commander of the Fourth Army, to liaise with the Third Army commander, General Sir Edmund 'Bloody Bull' Allenby, to conduct a thorough feasibility study of such an offence, in a combined operation with the French astride the Somme, employing some twenty-five divisions.

The great bend of the meandering River Somme and its tributary, the Ancre, bisects a rolling, undulating tableland dotted with hamlets and fed by a myriad of shallow streams. Nowhere does the countryside rise above 500ft.

Early in April, Rawlinson forwarded a plan to General Headquarters. With the limited resources that he had been informed would be at his disposal, the general made it clear that he would not be able to deal effectively with an objective with a width exceeding 20,000yd, and with a depth of a maximum of 5,000yd. He addressed the options of a single mass assault on the German positions, or a series of staged advances. He also favoured a sustained, methodical artillery bombardment lasting up to seventy-two hours as opposed to a short intense barrage. Rawlinson opined that if the artillery did their job well, then the rest would be easy.

After detailed consultation with his French counterpart, General Joseph 'Papa' Joffre, it was agreed that the offensive should not take place beyond the end of June.

In his despatch, Haig, who would go on to earn, perhaps unfairly, the sobriquet 'the Butcher of the Somme', wrote:

> Vast stocks of ammunition and stores of all kinds had to be accumulated beforehand within a convenient distance of our front. To deal with these, many miles of new railways – both standard and narrow gauge – and trench tramways were laid. All available roads were improved, many others were made, and long causeways were built over marshy valleys.
>
> Many additional dug-outs had to be provided as shelter for the troops, for use as dressing stations for the wounded, and as magazines for storing ammunition, food, water and engineering material.
>
> Scores of miles of deep communication trenches had to be dug, as well as trenches for telephone wires, assembly and assault trenches, and numerous gun emplacements and observation posts.

British 6in howitzer. (Photo Gerry van Tonder)

rman 10.5cm howitzer. (Photo Gerry van Tonder)

Important mining operations were undertaken, and charges were laid at various points beneath the enemy's lines.

Except in the river valleys the existing supplies of water were hopelessly insufficient to meet the requirements of the numbers of men and horses to be concentrated in this area as the preparations for our offensive proceeded. To meet this difficulty many wells and borings were sunk, and over 100 pumping plants were installed. More than 100 miles of water mains were laid, and everything was got ready to ensure an adequate water supply as our troops advanced.

> (Sir J.A. Hammerton, Ed., *A Popular History of the Great War,*
> Vol. 3 *The Allies at Bay: 1916,* Fleetwood House, London, 1916)

Part of Haig's plan was to lengthen the front northwards with a subsidiary offensive against the German stronghold at Gommecourt, a task given to VII Corps under Lieutenant General Sir Thomas D'Oyly Snow. The corps was composed of the 56th Division (Major General C.P.H. Hull), the 37th Division (Major General Lord Edward Gleichen) and the 46th (North Midland) Division commanded by Montagu-Stuart-Wortley. Of the three brigades in the 46th Division – 137th, 138th, 139th – the Robin Hoods' brigade, the 139th, was the farthest north (see map in the colour section).

The 46th had to open the attack in this sector with a thrust to the northern, wooded German salient at Gommecourt. The enemy position was deemed impregnable to a frontal attack, so the Midlands troops would sweep round the north while the London troops completed the pincer move to the south.

The importance that the Germans attached to this position 'may be gathered from the fact that it was held by part of the 2nd Guards Reserve Division – picked troops numbering 1,295 rifles and 11 machine guns, with 56 rifles and 1 machine gun in support'.

German machine-gun nest. (Photo Sendker)

At this time, Commanding Officer Colonel Brewill withdrew to England on medical grounds – the 'exacting strain of a long period of responsibility'. Major Lawrence Arthur Hind stepped into the extremely demanding position of commander of the Robin Hoods.

On 19 May, the Robin Hoods relieved a battalion from the 137th Brigade in the trenches west of Foncquevillers, getting their first feel of the sector from which their fateful assault on Gommecourt would be launched in six weeks' time.

On 3 June, the battalion was relieved and, three days later, marched in torrential rain at night to Sus-Saint-Léger. Here they immediately commenced such rigorous training for the attack a month hence, that some of the Tommies complained that the trenches were easier. A mock-up of the enemy position had been constructed, clearly marked with machine-gun emplacements, dugouts and observation posts.

> It must be acknowledged that the equipment and preparation of the English attack were magnificent ... The Officers were provided with excellent maps which shewed every German trench systematically named, and gave every detail of our positions. The sketches had been brought up to date with all our latest work.
>
> (Official German report captured a few months after the Battle of the Somme)

The Robin Hoods moved to Bienvillers, 'fit down to the last-joined man, splendidly trained for the offensive work in hand, high in morale; in a word – ready for anything'.

British 9.45in trench
mortar. (Photo Gerry
van Tonder)

German 7.6cm trench mortar. (Photo Gerry van Tonder)

For the next ten days, however, the battalion stagnated in the terrible conditions the found on their arrival. Lieutenant Colonel Arthur W. Brewill expands:

> Guns were everywhere ... they stood wheel to wheel. Heavy rains and the constant procession of guns and ammunition had churned the roads into muddy furrows. On every side were signs of the offensive. The enemy artillery and our own kept up an intermittent but lively duel.
>
> In the Communication trenches and Fire trenches it was difficult to find a place where the muddy water came below the knees, and for long stretches it was up to the thighs.
>
> The effects of this disastrous weather were far-reaching; they were, in fact, a deciding factor in the attack. Large sections of trenches collapsed altogether, their sides simply sliding in, being undermined by the water. Bomb shelters, ammunition dumps, ration stores, &c., fared likewise.

The reader will understand something of the problem confronting the staff, as to ho to get the sector ready for the attack, when only ten days remained. Needless to say the Herculean task never was accomplished. But why the attacking battalion was chosen this work remains a mystery that can only be explained by those in authority. Finding la working parties, fighting and reconnoitring patrols every night in drenching rain, reduced the strength of the battalion, and lessened the chances of success in the forthcoming attack.

In preparation for the attack, 250 men of the Robin Hoods assisted with the digging of a 'jumping-off' trench about 140yd forward of the front line and almost half way across no man's land.

> During the night the enemy dug a new trench about 250 metres in front of the right flank of the Regimental Sector, N. of the Gommecourt–Foncquevillers Road. Wire not yet up.
>
> (German War Diary, Saturday, 26 June 1916)

On the nights of 28 and 29 June, the Robin Hoods sent out two patrols, each comprising two officers and thirty-two soldiers. One patrol was tasked with ascertaining the effect of the British artillery bombardment on the Greman trenches, while the other was to closely examine the enemy wire to see if, as had been reported, the artillery had 'adequately cut' the enemy barbed-wire defences to allow rapid passage through the entanglement during the assault.

Friday, June 30th
9.15 a.m. No signs of attack.
9.45 a.m. The impression of an attack on Gommecourt as being imminent is not confirmed from the right sector.

…o the night. (Photo John Warwick Brooke)

2.30 p.m. An English prisoner makes the following statement: 'No black troops present – no gas, nothing known about attack.' Prisoner was leading a patrol to ascertain effect of bombardment on our trenches.

5.45 p.m. Several gaps have been made in enemy's wire close together on a breadth of 15 metres. One other rank killed. 11 other ranks wounded.

(German War Diary)

After two rain-induced postponements, H-hour was finally set for 7.30 am, 1 July 1916.

At 9.00 pm the night before, after 'just two simple prayers ... the voice of the padre half-drowned by the din of the guns', the Robin Hood platoons started filing down the flooded trenches towards the front. The Carrying Company arrived an hour late, their progress severely hampered by the muddy quagmire and fearful of losing their loads into the mud. Every time there was a stoppage in their painfully slow and tedious slog, 'their legs became firmly embedded in the lower strata of mud, and were only extracted with the greatest difficulty'.

As it started getting light, the German artillery commenced laying down a heavy barrage on the British trenches, drawing an equal response from the British artillery.

Saturday, July 1st

The intense bombardment shortly before the attack, succeeded in rendering the front trenches in G.1. and G.5. ripe for the assault ... It was then evident that the main attack would be directed North and South of Gommecourt village, in order to cut off the garrison of Gommecourt.

(German War Diary)

German 21cm howitzer. (Photo Gerry van Tonder)

The attack by the Robin Hoods would be in five company-based waves. The first four waves comprised A Company under Captain T.H. Leman, B Company under Lieutenant J. Macpherson, and C Company under Captain A.A. Walton. D Company, commanded by Captain W.H. Round, would follow with his carrying and digging company.

At 7.27 am, smoke was discharged, but the resultant thick screen caused a loss of visible direction.

At 7.30 am, the first wave went 'over the top' of the newly dug advance trench, while the second and third waves clambered out of their old trench. The fourth wave charged out from the first's retrenchment, while the fifth wave came up 'Green Street' trench. Colonel Brewill continues:

> Immediately, the enemy opened with a heavy and accurate shell and machine gun barrage on our front line and wire, which practically annihilated the 3rd and 4th waves. A few survivors heroically pressed on. The Carrying Company was much hindered coming up the Communication Trench, and did not get over until 8 a.m. By that time the wind had changed and most of the smoke was over our own trenches; No-man's land was quite clear from 70 yards in front of our trenches up to the enemy's lines. The Carrying Company pushed on but lost very heavily.

Only twelve men of the battalion reached the German second line, but, finding themselves alone and isolated, were forced to fall back to the enemy's first line. Only five men were successful. Here they found twenty-four of their brothers-in-arms, but they could offer very little resistance against the enemy's onslaught. The Germans made bombing attacks on both flanks, while the trapped Robin Hoods had exhausted their own supply of bombs. The muddy water had also rendered several rifles unserviceable. Eventually, the few remaining who could still physically move, crawled into shell holes immediately in front of the German wire.

> The enemy's attack, which was made under cover of gas bombs was perceived ... the shell holes were occupied exactly at the right moment and the attackers were received with hand grenades. The barrage fire which had been called for began at once.
>
> The enemy built up his firing line and attempted to press forward with bombers and flame projectors, but was repulsed everywhere.
>
> (German War Diary)

Meanwhile, battalion bombing officer, Lieutenant C.H. Burton, led a small party close to the German third line, but realizing they lacked support of any form, Burton, badly wounded, was compelled to retire to the enemy's first line, but only after firing several rifle grenades at the German trench. Upon reaching the German first line, Burton found Captain Leman who, although twice wounded and weak, was trying to organize a defence. After exhausting their supply of bombs, at last light the remaining six survivors, moving from one shell hole to another, arrived back at their lines in the dark. The 21-year-old Leman succumbed to his wounds.

Casualties mount. (Photo Ernest Brooks)

In these early stages of the attack, the Robin Hoods lost their newly appointed commanding officer, Lieutenant Colonel Lawrence Arthur Hind MC, and the battalion adjutant, Captain Roby Middleton Gotch. Colonel Brewill again:

> As far as can be ascertained these two officers proceeded with the first wave and passed over No Man's Land to within 50 yards of the German trenches. Taking shelter in a shell hole, the C.O. raised himself on his hands and knees to look for a place in the wire entanglements where he could get through, and in doing this he was shot through the forehead and immediately dropped. Private Tomlinson who was lying in the same shell hole at once went to him, but found that death had been instantaneous.

The much-loved and respected Captain Round of the supporting D Company was also killed. Owing to the mud, the company suffered unavoidable but costly delays in going forward. Sustaining high levels of casualties, repeated attempts by the men to go out to their comrades failed.

Battalion medical officer, Captain Scott, led a party behind the fourth wave, but about seventy yards from their trenches they found themselves in the open, immediately attracting German fire. Only 'one or two' made it back unwounded.

> The English enfilading guns fired with such accuracy that every round fell actually into the trenches ... rendering the line untenable. The Infantry assault was perceived only when the enfilade fire on the trench was lifted beyond the parados [back of the trench], and simultaneously the English bombers appeared on the parapet.

Even the tunnelled dugouts, which were six metres deep, could not keep out the heavy 15 inch shells: they were blown in. All the trenches bombarded on July 1st were completely flattened out. Only shell holes remained.

The English had excellent maps of our trenches. They were extremely well-equipped with bridging ladders, equipment for close fighting, obstacles, machine guns and rations; they were well acquainted with the use of our hand-grenades.

Our own barrage fire opened promptly and was very effective. The enemy's barrage often failed.

(German War Diary)

For the pride of Nottingham, the 1/7th (Robin Hood) Battalion, the Sherwood Foresters, it was the greatest, single tragedy that had ever befallen the regiment. On that day, 27 officers and 600 other ranks launched themselves at the Germans at Gommecourt – 90 returned. At La Bazeque Farm, a small number of officers, NCOs and men remained behind to form the nucleus of a new battalion should this prove necessary – events would prove that this was a fortuitous precaution.

An amazing story is recorded of a battalion officer, Lieutenant S.E. Barnwell, who crawled back into their trench four days after having been reported missing. Exhausted and his clothes in tatters, Barnwell had been wounded in seven places. For the duration of his absence, he had lain in no man's land without food and water, except for what he could scavenge from the dead around him. In his exposed position, he was constantly fired on by German snipers.

In the early hours of 2 July, the ragged remnants of the battalion were relieved, marching to Warlincourt via Bienvillers. Only six officers remained unwounded. On 6 July, Lieutenant Colonel W.S.N. Toller was appointed commanding officer of the Robin Hoods.

The ruins of Gommecourt Château. (Photo Ernest Brooks)

The names of 155 Robin Hoods are inscribed on the massive Thiepval Anglo-French memorial on the Ancre in France, their bodies never found, and 'to whom the fortune of war denied the known and honoured burial given to their comrades in death'.

According to regimental war diary statistics of the time, the Robin Hood casualties for all ranks on the first day of the Somme offensive were:

Killed in action 46
Missing, believed killed in action 34
Missing, believed wounded in action 10
Missing 118
Wounded 196
Wounded at duty 39
Total 443

German military reports show the following casualties suffered on the same day:

Killed in action 185
Missing 24
Wounded 382
Total 591

On 3 March 1917, the Robin Hoods found themselves 'back in the trenches in front of Foncquevillers', where the 8th Sherwood Foresters held a position 'running diagonally across Gommecourt Park'. The next night, strong patrols from A, B and C companies moved into 'the Z', their primary objective eight long months previously. As they entered the sector, the enemy was completing its withdrawal.

Over the next few days, the Robin Hoods scoured the old no man's land, searching for the bodies of their comrades who had fallen on the first day of the Somme offensive. The decomposed bodies of captains Thomas Henry Leman and William Eaton Guy Walker and second lieutenants Wilfred Ernest Flint and Frank Burfield Gamble were discovered on uncut wire in front of Gommecourt Park. There was no trace of any of the other officers.

They are among the twenty-one soldiers of the Robin Hoods who fell on 1 July 1916 and who are interred in the Commonwealth War Graves Commission's Foncqueviller Military Cemetery.

Second World War, El Alamein

When I assumed command of the Eighth Army I said that the mandate was to destroy Rommel and his army, and that it would be done as soon as we were ready.

We are ready *now*.

The battle which is now about to begin will be one of the decisive battles of history. It will be the turning-point of the war. The eyes of the whole world will be on us, watching anxiously which way the battle will swing.

We can give them an answer at once: It will swing our way.

We have first-class equipment, good tanks, good anti-tank guns, plenty of artillery and plenty of ammunition, and we are backed by the finest air striking force in the world.

Therefore, let every officer and man enter the battle with a stout heart and with the determination to do his duty so long as he has breath in his body.

> (Lieutenant General Bernard Montgomery
> to his troops on the eve of the Second Battle of El Alamein)

Encouraged by Hitler's remarkable blitzkrieg successes in Western Europe, Italian dictator Benito Mussolini developed a vision of a latter-day Roman empire across the north of Africa, stretching from Libya to Eritrea, evicting the British from Egypt in the process and laying claim to the rich oilfields of the Persian Gulf.

Losing the Suez Canal, however, was not an option for Britain. The consequences of an Italian-controlled Suez – Britain's lifeline to India – and losing the port of Alexandria, was too serious to even contemplate. So, for the three years following Italian Marshal Rodolfo Graziani's invasion of Egypt in September 1940, the Western Desert became a theatre of seesawing fortunes as the German *Panzerarmee Afrika* and the British Eighth Army locked horns in a series of armour-dominated battles, the magnitude of which never before seen in the history of warfare.

In October 1942, Lieutenant General Bernard Montgomery won one of the most decisive battles of the Second World War, defeating Axis forces at the strategic town of El Alamein. British Prime Minister Churchill could at last boast of a turning point in Allied fortunes in North Africa.

Montgomery planned to lay down an extremely heavy artillery barrage before sending in four infantry divisions to force breaks in the German–Italian line for his armour. Montgomery's main thrust was to the north, in a parallel line ten miles south of the Mediterranean coast.

The infantry divisions of XXX Corps would be used, supported by X Armoured Corps. X Armoured Corps was made up of the 1st Armoured Division, commanded at the time by Major General Raymond Briggs, and the 10th Armoured Division under Major General Alexander Gatehouse. One of the armoured brigades in this division was the 8th, formed in 1941, which consisted of:

3rd Royal Tank Regiment
Sherwood Rangers Yeomanry

Afrika Korps commander,
Field Marshal Erwin Romme

Staffordshire Yeomanry (Queen's Own Royal Regiment)
1st Battalion, Buffs (Royal East Kent Regiment)
1st Regiment, Royal Horse Artillery
97th (Kent Yeomanry) Field Regiment, Royal Artillery

The Sherwood Rangers Yeomanry was raised in 1794 as the Nottinghamshire Yeoman
Cavalry.

An 1899 Royal Warrant, issued in the wake of a string of humiliating defeats in Sou
Africa, permitted volunteer forces to serve in that theatre during the Anglo-Boer War.
response, the regiment supplied the 10th (Sherwood Rangers) Company, numbering ju
over 110 troops.

At the outbreak of the Great War, the Sherwood Rangers consisted of four squadro·
based at Newark, Mansfield, Worksop and Retford. Restructured into three line re
ments, the Sherwood Rangers adopted a largely cavalry role during the conflict.

Between the wars, the efficacy of horsed cavalry in combat now obsolete, several Brit.
yeomanry regiments were moved to the Royal Tank Corps as armoured car companies,

Badajoz 6 April 1812

Key

- Forts
- French mines
- False attacks
- British artillery batteries
- British movements
- British parallel trenches

River Guadiana

Parallel May/June
French redoubt
Fort San Cristobal
Fort Tetre de Pont
Picton
No 12 Bty
No 8 Bty
Badajoz
No 4 Bty
No 10 Bty
No 11 Bty
No 3 Bty
No 2 Bty
No 1 Bty
False attack
on 6 April
Engineer
Park

Fort Pardaleras
Leith
Light
Barnard
Colville

False attack
on 6 April

French Strongholds
1 San Vicente
2 San José
3 Santiago
4 San Juan
5 San Roque
6 Santa Maria
7 Trinidad
8 San Pedro

Tower musket as used in the battle

Shako plate

British artillery 9-pounder gun

British artillery 24-pounder gun

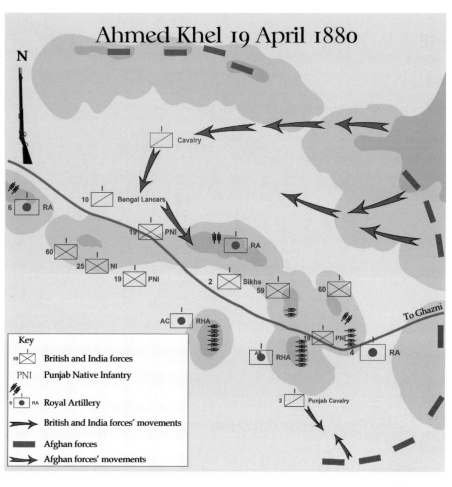

Ahmed Khel 19 April 1880

N

Cavalry

6 RA

10 Bengal Lancers

19 PNI

60

25 NI

19 PNI

RA

2 Sikhs

59

60

AC RHA

19 PNI

AB RHA

4 RA

To Ghazni

2 Punjab Cavalry

Key

59 ⊠	British and India forces
PNI	Punjab Native Infantry
6 ● RA	Royal Artillery
→	British and India forces' movements
▬	Afghan forces
⇒	Afghan forces' movements

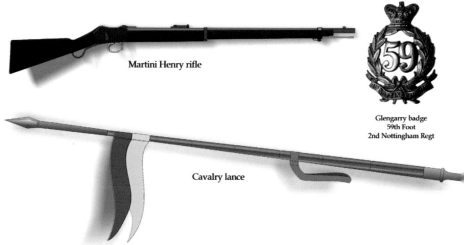

Martini Henry rifle

Cavalry lance

Glengarry badge
59th Foot
2nd Nottingham Regt

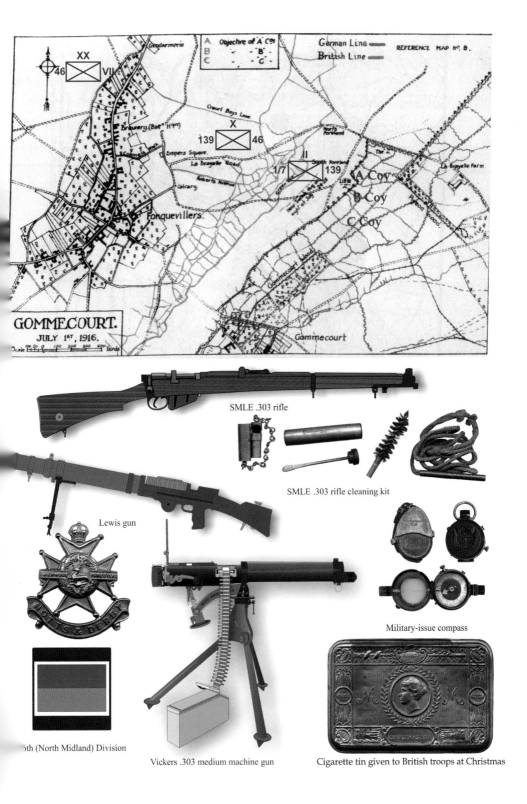

GOMMECOURT.

JULY 1ST, 1916.

SMLE .303 rifle

SMLE .303 rifle cleaning kit

Lewis gun

Military-issue compass

5th (North Midland) Division

Vickers .303 medium machine gun

Cigarette tin given to British troops at Christmas

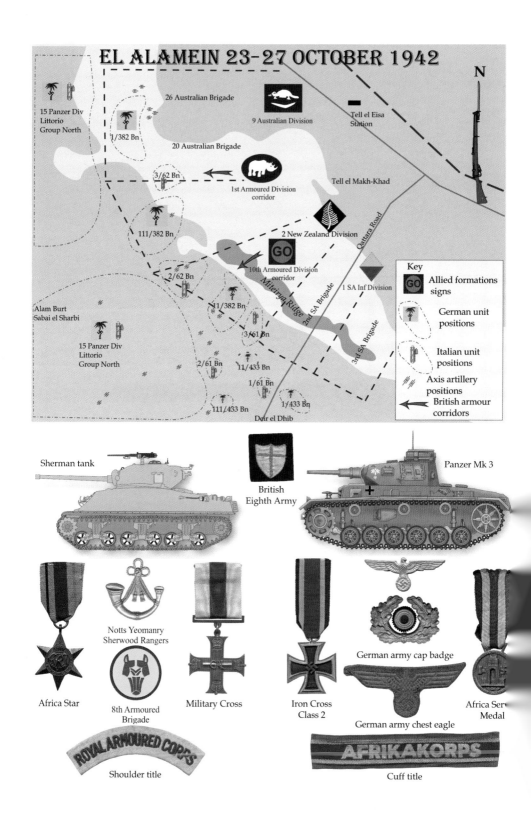

EL ALAMEIN 23-27 OCTOBER 1942

N

15 Panzer Div
Littorio
Group North

26 Australian Brigade

9 Australian Division

Tell el Eisa
Station

1/382 Bn

20 Australian Brigade

3/62 Bn

1st Armoured Division
corridor

Tell el Makh-Khad

111/382 Bn

2 New Zealand Division

Qattara Road

GO

10th Armoured Division
corridor

Miteiriya Ridge

2nd SA Brigade

1 SA Inf Division

2/62 Bn

Alam Burt
Sabai el Sharbi

11/382 Bn

3/61 Bn

3rd SA Brigade

15 Panzer Div
Littorio
Group North

2/61 Bn

11/433 Bn

1/61 Bn

111/433 Bn

1/433 Bn

Deir el Dhib

Key

GO — Allied formations signs

German unit positions

Italian unit positions

Axis artillery positions

← British armour corridors

Sherman tank

British
Eighth Army

Panzer Mk 3

Notts Yeomanry
Sherwood Rangers

Africa Star

8th Armoured
Brigade

Military Cross

Iron Cross
Class 2

German army cap badge

German army chest eagle

Africa Serv
Medal

ROYAL ARMOURED CORPS

Shoulder title

AFRIKAKORPS

Cuff title

Captain Albert Ball VC, DSO & two Bars, MC

2/7th (Robin Hood) Bn
Sherwood Foresters
cap badge

Royal Flying Corps
cap badge

Royal Aircraft Factory S.E.5 flown by Captain Albert Ball

Decorations and medals awarded to Captain Albert Ball VC, DSO & two Bars, MC

Plaques of Nottinghamshire regimental badges at the Courts of Justice. (Photos Gerry van Tonder)

Private Derby, Royal Mercian Regiment mascot (left), and his service medals and coat with regimer battle honours. (Photos the Mercian Regiment)

Above left: Notts and Derby soldiers on parade, 1913. (Painting by Ernest Ibbotson)

Above right: Worcestershire and Sherwood Foresters, Windsor Castle guard. (Photo Philip Allfrey)

...erwood Rangers monument, Groesbeek, near Nijmegen, to those of the regiment who died ...hting the Germans in Holland in the Second World War. The tank, donated by the Notts Sherwood ...ngers Yeomanry, is a Grizzly-1, a Canadian-built M4A1 Sherman tank with some modifications.

Machine Gun Platoon, Support Company
1st Battalion The Worcestershire and
Sherwood Foresters, in training.
(Photo MOD)

105mm L118 light guns. (Photo MOD)

absorbed into other signals and infantry battalions. Two others were disbanded, while a further twenty-five regiments became brigades in the Royal Field Artillery. The Sherwood Rangers, however, were retained as mounted cavalry, a status still maintained at the Second World War mobilization in 1939.

As part of the 5th Cavalry Brigade, the Sherwood Rangers were briefly deployed to the British mandate of Palestine, before undergoing conversion in 1940 to artillery. The latest transformation introduced the Nottinghamshire troops to North Africa's Western Desert campaign where, in their new role of artillery, they participated in the defence of Tobruk and Benghazi.

The following year, the Sherwood Rangers was converted to armour and posted to the 8th Armoured Brigade, where they were initially equipped with M3 Grant and M4 Sherman tanks, and the British Crusader 'cruise' tank. The latter was also referred to as cavalry tank, essentially designed as fast-moving armoured and mechanized cavalry.

By nightfall on 23 October 1942, tens of thousands of troops from Montgomery's Eighth Army lay concealed in the jumping-off positions facing the German and Italian positions just south of El Alamein (see map in the colour section).

At 21h40 to the second, a wide half-moon of flashes rent the night sky to the zenith. An instant later, the ear-splitting crash of that perfectly coordinated fire order tumbled from the sky. Backward and forward the guns flickered and flashed as battery after battery opened fire. For 20 minutes the mighty artillery concentration roared and hammered in deafening chorus. The sound of thousands of shells falling on the enemy was like the sound of a hailstorm on a city of corrugated iron or the rumble of ten thousand drums. It was appalling.

...usader tank, Western
...sert, October 1942.
...oto Sgt Neill)

At the same instant [as mortar batteries started firing] a regiment of heavy machine guns began to add their shrill clamour to the now almost indescribable uproar. Half a million rounds were to pour from the Vickers muzzles before 'Cease fire!' In a few moments it was impossible to distinguish between the different weapons. It was simply an awful roaring which battered on eardrums protected by cotton wool.

(James Ambrose Brown, *Retreat to Victory: A Springbok's Diary in North Africa, Gazala to El Alamein 1942,* Ashanti Publishing, Johannesburg, 1991)

Early reports from the north indicated that XXX Corps was making satisfactory progress, while to the south, infantry from the 51st Highland, New Zealand and 1st South African divisions were resolutely penetrating Miteiriya Ridge to clear a corridor for the 10th Armoured Division.

At 2.00 am on the morning of the 24th, sappers led the Sherwood Rangers along a track towards the corridor, their route through the minefields demarcated with burning tins of petrol and tape, punctuated with regular control posts.

An hour before first light, and running behind schedule, nine Crusader tanks of A Squadron, Sherwood Rangers, entered the minefield. After only a mile, the enemy expressed its dissatisfaction with the presence of the Allied armour. Trooper Philip Forester of A Squadron relates:

As dawn broke the flood of battle burst with staccato fury. The tanks had fallen foul of savage cross fire from 88mm guns and machine guns. Everywhere there was a criss-crossing of coloured tracer, accompanied by the ear-splitting crescendo of explosion, and the bark of small arms fire. Green, red, and whitish balls of brilliant fire raced through the air at colossal speed, seeking their targets. The whole column on the track through the minefield had been forced to halt owing to this powerful opposition. Tanks began to 'brew up' [also called 'Tommy cookers', when a tank bursts into flame when hit] right and left. I glanced forward at other lines of tanks extended in battle order like ships of a fleet. It was extraordinary how in this half-light of dawn these armoured monsters suggested the sil-houettes of battleships floating dispassionately in a calm sea. Armoured piercing thermite shells ricocheted close to the echelon, cracking viciously as they smacked the deck.

A Squadron bore the brunt of the German fire, but still managed to knock out two enem tanks. B Squadron, now clear of the minefield, also sustained losses. As day dawned, th Sherwood Rangers had lost sixteen tanks, forcing the regiment to pull slightly back dug-in infantry on Miteiriya Ridge to regroup and hold their position. Here the troo and armour had to withstand a withering onslaught from the German artillery.

That night, the 24th, the Sherwoods held the ridge until being pulled back the follo ing night. In that 24-hour period, they repelled two German counter-attacks, all the whi taking persistent and aggressive artillery and aerial bombardment. Rommel's 15th Panz Division threw a hundred tanks at the ridge, their thrust centring on the Sherwoods, which the regiment opened up with everything they had. Their commander, Lieutena Colonel Edward 'Flash' Kellet (killed in action 22 March 1943) called down smoke to silho ette the enemy armour, but the smoke obscured the enemy advance from the 9th Armour Brigade 2,000yd to south-west, thereby preventing them from rendering immediate ass tance. In spite of this, and with the smoke discontinued, the enemy was driven off.

An M3 Grant tank
crew inspects a
knocked-out German
Panzerkampfwagen
I light tank variant.
(Photo Capt G. Keating)

Enemy bombers wreaked havoc on the ridge, destroying much of the echelon and its
fuel and ammunition support vehicles. Such was the sheer ferocity of the German attack
on the position that the 8th Armoured Brigade failed to reach its planned objective.

The Sherwood Rangers suffered eighty-five casualties, including all the officers of
A Squadron, in the first two days of Montgomery's offensive, codenamed Operation Lightfoot.
The regiment lost half its tanks and all of its echelon. The 10th Armoured Division losses as at
21 October amounted to 1,350, the equivalent of 50 per cent of the tank crews.

On 28 October, the 8th Armoured Brigade resumed its position in the line at Kidney
Ridge, relieving the 1st Armoured Division.

From then until 1 November, the Sherwood Rangers were engaged in several skirmishes, while Montgomery increased his infantry strengths to the north in a concerted
push towards the Mediterranean. This also had the hoped-for outcome of drawing
Rommel's reserves to the north to counter Montgomery's initiative. This in turn relieved
pressure on the 1st Armoured Division's centre line.

In preparation for Operation Supercharge, the 8th Armoured Brigade briefly fell under
the command of the 1st Armoured Division.

On 2 November, Montgomery swung directly to the west as he launched Operation
Supercharge, punching through the now weakened German–Italian line. Combined with
further Eighth Army offensives from the south, by mid-January 1943, Rommel with his
Afrika Korps had been pushed through Libya and into Tunisia, effectively marking the
end of the Axis hold over the Western Desert. Ebullient Prime Minister Churchill was
prompted to say, 'Up to Alamein we survived. After Alamein, we conquered.'

Lloyd tracked personnel carrier used in the Western Desert campaigns. (Photo Gerry van Tonder)

On 23 January, the 3rd Royal Tank Regiment followed the 11th Hussars into the Libyan coastal city of Tripoli. The next day, a combined force made up of the Sherwood Rangers Yeomanry, 1st Buffs, 5th Regiment, Royal Horse Artillery and 7th Medium Regiment, Royal Artillery, advanced to the Zavia area, south-west of Tripoli. Here, the brigade was rested pending the commencement of the Tunisian Campaign. The brigade would take up an offensive position at the Mareth Line, a twenty-eight-mile-long system of concrete fortification built by the French in 1936, and now garrisoned by German and Italian infantry and armour.

At this stage, the 8th Armoured Division was restructured and provided with new equipment. Three armoured regimental groups were formed for the new-look brigade the 3rd Royal Tank Regiment, the Staffordshire Yeomanry and the Sherwood Ranger (Nottinghamshire Yeomanry).

The Sherwoods were now equipped with twenty-three Sherman, four Grant and nineteen Crusader tanks, and six armoured cars. The infantry element was provided b A Company, the 1st Buffs.

On 14 March, the brigade was passed to the command of the New Zealand Corps, when it joined the 2nd New Zealand Division, the Free French, General Philippe Leclerc of Hauteclocque's 'L' Force from Chad, and the 1st Free French Brigade. Following an unsuccessful attempt by XXX Corps to dislodge the enemy in a frontal attack on the Mareth Line, the New Zealand Corps was tasked with outflanking enemy positions in Operation Supercharge II.

Towards the end of March, the 8th Armoured Brigade thrust deep into the Switch Line in the direction of El Hamma. The Axis forces withdrew sixty miles to the north-west Wadi Akarit where the Sherwoods encountered the much-feared *Panzerkampfwagen* Tiger tank.

Daimler Mk I armoured car, North Africa. (Photo Gerry van Tonder)

The Sherwoods ended their North African tour of duty after battles at Enfidaville and Takrouna and the capitulation of the Axis in North Africa on 13 May. The weary Sherwoods gradually made their way back to Egypt to await transport home, arriving in England on 9 December.

The Sherwood Rangers were then granted a period of extended leave before commencing training for the 6 June 1944 Allied invasion of Normandy.

4. THEY SERVED

Over many centuries, the citizenry of Nottingham – and indeed the whole county – was never found wanting when a call to the colours was broadcast. Given the confines of space of this historical work, this is but a miniscule representative fraction of those who served and served well.

Colonel John Hutchinson (1615–1664)

[Hutchinson:] My lord, hearing that there were some question concerning the county's powder, I am come to kiss your lordship's hands, and to beseech you that I may know what your desires and intents are concerning it!

[Newark:] Cousin, the king desires to borrow it of the country, to supply his great necessities.

[Hutchinson:] I beseech your lordship, what commission have you to demand this?

[Newark:] Upon my honour, I have a commission from his majesty, but it is left behind me; but I will engage my honour it shall be repaid the country.

[Hutchinson:] Your lordship's honour as an engagement, would be accepted for more than I am worth; but in such an occasion as this, the greatest man's engagement in, the kingdom, cannot be a satisfaction to the country.

[Newark:] The king's intents are only to borrow it, and if the country will not lend it, he will pay for it.

[Hutchinson:] My lord, it is not the value of the powder we endeavour to preserve, but in times of danger, as these are, those things which serve for our defence, are not valuable at any price, should you give as many barrels of gold as you take barrels of powder.

[Newark:] Upon my faith and honour, cousin, it shall be restored in ten days.

[Hutchinson:] My lord, such is the danger of the times, that for aught we know, we may in less than four days be ruined for want of it; and I beseech your lordship to consider how sad a thing it is in these times of war, to leave a poor country and the people in it, naked and open to the injury of every passenger; for if you take our powder, you may as well take our arms, without which we are unable to make use of them, and I hope your lord-ship will not disarm the country.

[Newark:] Why, who should the country fear? I am their lord-lieutenant, and engaged with my life and honour to defend them! What danger are they in?

[Hutchinson:] Danger! yes, my lord, great danger; there is a troop of horse now in the town, and it hath often happened so that they have committed great outrages and insolencies, calling divers honest men puritans and rogues, with divers other provoking terms and carriages.

[August 1642, Sir John Digby was high sheriff and Lord Newark the Lord Lieutenant.]

(Rev Julius Hutchinson, *Memoirs of The Life of Colonel Hutchinson, Governor of Nottingham Castle and Town*, Henry G. Bohn, London, Tenth Edition, 1863)

In August 1642, with the towns and villages of the Midlands divided in their loyalties between Royalists and Parliamentarians, the 32-year-old Colonel John Hutchinson of Owthorpe Hall, staunch Parliamentarian and commander of Nottingham's Parliamentarian garrison, refused to acquiesce to Lord Lieutenant Lord Newark's demands for him (Hutchinson) to hand over to him the contents of the Nottingham powder magazine.

Educated at Nottingham and Lincoln grammar schools, and at Cambridge before entering Lincoln's Inn to study law, Hutchinson instead followed his greatest life's desires: divinity and music.

Like his father, Sir Thomas, Hutchinson was also an MP in the Long Parliament, representing Nottinghamshire. By order of the town committee, and steered by Sir John Meldrum, in June 1643 Hutchinson took up command of Nottingham Castle.

In November that year, Scottish peer and fellow MP, Lord Fairfax of Cameron, commissioned Hutchinson to raise a regiment of foot. Finally, parliament appointed Hutchinson governor of both Nottingham and its castle.

The town continued to attract the attentions of the king's forces, but Hutchinson remained doggedly steadfast. Refusing to entertain any offers of surrender, in January 1644 he dealt with Royalist commander Sir Charles Lucas's troops who had managed to enter the town to try to set it to the torch. Four years later, Lucas was found guilty of treason and shot to death in Colchester Castle.

Notwithstanding continuous acrimony between the town committee and its governor, who had a reputation for being a loose cannon, in March 1964 Hutchinson was returned to parliament.

Colonel John Hutchinson.

In January 1949, Hutchinson was appointed as one of the 135 commissioners – judges – to hear the case of treason against King Charles I. As expected, Charles was found guilty. Hutchinson and fifty-eight of the other commissioners signed the king's death warrant.

In 1660, after political upheaval that followed the death of Oliver Cromwell in 1658, who had been head of the English Commonwealth (Interregnum), Charles II reclaimed the English throne. He immediately set about a programme of reconciliation to settle the instability in his realm, actions which were enshrined in the Indemnity and Oblivion Act (1660).

Hutchinson received a Royal pardon, but 104 of his fellow commissioners were named and listed as not entitled to reprieve. A varied tranche of 'sentences' were imposed on the commissioners, or regicides as they became known. Some were just hanged, others hanged, drawn and quartered, while others faced life in prison. Twenty-four commissioners who were no longer alive, including Cromwell, were given posthumous death sentences. Their bodies were exhumed, hanged and beheaded, the severed heads placed on spikes in public places.

In October 1663, Hutchinson was implicated in the Farnley Wood Plot to overthrow the monarchy. The government's case lacked substance, but they finally had the opportunity to imprison the 'traitor'.

Hutchinson was incarcerated in the Tower of London, pending a warrant for his transportation to the Isle of Man. In May 1664, however, he was taken to Sandown Castle in Kent where he was locked up in atrocious conditions.

St Margaret's Church, Owthorpe, the Nottinghamshire family seat where John Hutchinson was laid to rest. (Photo Gerry van Tonder)

Four months later, Hutchinson's health failed and he died of fever. His wife, Lucy, ironically the daughter of Sir Allen Apsley, Lord Lieutenant of the Tower of London, was granted permission to remove his body to the family seat in Owthorpe, where he was interred in St Margaret's Church.

Admiral Sir John Borlase Warren GCB, GCH, PCH (1753–1822)

On Monday se'nnight the Nottingham volunteer cavalry and infantry had their first field day, on which occasion that brave admiral, Sir John Borlase Warren, appeared in the ranks as a sergeant, having enrolled himself as one of the first institution of the association'.

(*Stamford Mercury*, 3 May 1799)

Born in Stapleford, just over five miles from Nottingham, Warren's formative years were characterized by the pursuit of both an academic and a naval career. In April 1771, he enlisted in the Royal Navy as an able seaman, while graduating two years later with a BA degree from Emmanuel College, Cambridge. In 1776, Warren attained a master's degree, two years after he was first elected as the MP for Marlow in Buckinghamshire.

Warren performed his first tour of duty on the North American station, serving on board sloops and frigates during the American Revolutionary War of 1775–1783. During this period of his career, the ambitious Warren was twice promoted: to lieutenant in 1778 and captain in 1781.

On 23 April 1794, in command of a squadron of five frigates, Warren engaged a similar-sized French force about twenty-five nautical miles from Guernsey. Leading in his flagship *Flora*, and supported by *Arethusa*, after three hours of close-quarter action, the French frigates *Pomone* and *Babet* were compelled to surrender, suffering around 150 casualties. A while later, the French captain of the corvette *Engageante* conceded defeat – his ship was towed back to England. Britain enthused over this new hero, immediately making him a Knight of the Order of the Bath.

Spurred on by the profound gratitude of the Admiralty, in 1796 Warren was given command of another squadron of frigates, which he threw at the French coast, capturing 220 ships, including 37 of the French navy.

Admiral Sir John Borlase Warren. (Photo Gerry van Tonder)

LONDON, (Thursday) May 5

Extract of a Letter from NEWPORT, (Rhode Island) dated March 14, 1774, to the Master of the Rhode Island Coffee-House, LONDON.

'Sir, This Moment a Gentleman arrived from Boston, which Place he left Yesterday Morning, and informs, that on Monday Evening last a Number of Persons entered the Brig Fortune [two-masted sailing vessel], Capt. Gorham, who arrived from London on the preceding Day, and stove 28 and a half Chests of Tea, and discharged the Contents into the Harbour, being the whole of that Article which came in the said Vessel; no Damage was done to any other Goods.

The Inhabitants of Boston would have had the Tea returned to London, conformable to their Resolutions in December last, and the Customs-House Officers were waited upon, and requested to consent to its being returned; but the usual Obstacles being thrown in the Way, no Method was left to prevent the Introduction of that Dutied Article but the Destruction of it. This intelligence may be depended on.'

(*Derby Mercury*, Friday, 6 May 1774)

Off the west coast of Ireland on 10 October 1798, Warren, commanding a squadron of five frigates and three sail of the line, intercepted a French squadron carrying an invasion force of 5,000 soldiers. He captured four vessels and dispersed the rest. He received a gold medal from the Irish and British parliaments for averting a potential foreign invasion.

In February 1799, the 26-year-old Warren was promoted to the rank of rear admiral. Six years later he was made vice admiral, and on 31 July 1810, he became admiral. Warren was then returned to the Americas, where he was appointed commander-in-chief of the Halifax station. In August 1812, the Jamaica and Leeward Islands stations were amalgamated with Halifax to facilitate a single naval command and strategy during the American War of 1812.

Warren set up a blockade along the coast, employing ships from Bermuda and Halifax to patrol an extremely large stretch of American coastline from New York southwards. Added to this burdensome task was the provision of convoy protection between Jamaica and Quebec. Warren badgered the Admiralty for extra manpower, stores and materiel. Very likely after becoming annoyed with Warren's persistent requests, and much to his dissatisfaction, the Admiralty relieved Warren of his station.

It was only with the defeat of Napoleon early in 1814 that British naval forces were bolstered on the American east coast, thereby allowing purely defensive operations to take on a belligerent role. In an era where 'productivity bonuses' were the norm, Warren also faced loss of potential income that the capture of enemy ships attracted.

In 1815, Admiral Sir John Borlase Warren retired, a much-lauded hero in Nottinghamshire. On 27 February 1822, he died at Greenwich Hospital. He was interred in the family vault in Oxfordshire. Several pubs in Nottingham and county towns bear his name.

ıe French squadron engaged by Sir John Warren off the coast of Ireland in October 1798.
ainting by Nicholas Pocock)

lbert Ball, VC, DSO and Two Bars, MC (1896–1917)

CAPTAIN ALBERT BALL, D.S.O.

Famous Airman a Prisoner in Germany.

Captain Albert Ball, D.S.O., the famous airman who has brought down 42 enemies, and was reported missing, some time ago, is a prisoner in Germany.

Official news to this effect was received by his father, an ex-Mayor of Nottingham, from the War Office to-day. The news has given the greatest satisfaction, and shoals of congratulatory messages at the young hero's safety have been received from far and near.

(*Manchester Evening News*, Saturday, 19 May 1917)

bert Ball was born in Lenton – Sedgley House – Nottingham, on 14 August 1896, and tended Lenton Church School, Grantham Grammar School and Nottingham High, ·fore enrolling at Trent College. As a young teenager, Ball developed a passion for things echanical, while also becoming deeply religious.

On 21 September 1914, Ball enlisted in the 7th (Robin Hood) Battalion, the Sherwood ›resters (Nottinghamshire and Derbyshire Regiment). A month later, Ball received commission in the regiment as a subaltern, and was seconded to the North Midland .vision Cycle Company in January 1915.

In June, Ball commenced private flying lessons – usually before his army duties at 45 am – at Hendon Aerodrome. A year later, at his request, he was seconded for duty

Flying Officer Albert Ball.

with the Royal Flying Corps (RF
and given the rank of flying office
Receiving his wings on 26 Janua
1916, Ball was posted to No.
Squadron, RFC, in Marieux, Fran
where he flew the Royal Aircra
Factory B.E.2c on reconnaissance s
ties. Ball, however, became restle
with the unexciting and monotono
job of flying a two-seater witho
encountering any real action. Early
May, a delighted Ball was transferr
to No. 11 Squadron, RFC, a dedicat
fighter squadron operating Bristol I
'Biff' fighters and Royal Aircra
Factory F.E.2s.

By the time he was 18 years o
Ball had already been engaged
more than 100 dogfights, in which
brought down 29 German aircra
His daring exposed him to sever
narrow escapes, but he was nev
injured. In one scrap, his Lewis gu
out of ammunition, Ball flew alon
side the German aircraft where
shot and killed the hapless pilot wi
his revolver.

On 19 February 1917, the City of Nottingham bestowed the freedom of the city on Ba
in recognition of his astounding contribution as a flying officer in the war.

Ball was appointed temporary captain and flight commander in September 1916, b
the rank only became substantive a month after his death, his seniority backdated
30 November 1916.

On 6 May 1917, Ball took off on his final mission. Over the trenches of Douai ar
Cambrai, his squadron encountered elements of Baron Manfred von Richthofen's not
rious 'Flying Circus', during which both sides lost several aircraft. The last time Ball w
seen was as he was chasing a German aircraft into a bank of clouds.

Initially, unconfirmed reports were received indicating that Ball had been captur
alive by the Germans, but on 22 September 1917, the War Office issued a 'Certifica
of Death', a simple typed sheet of paper certifying that 'according to unofficial repor
received ... which are considered to be reliable, Captain Albert ... was killed in action
France of the 7th day of May, 1917'.

Ball had crashed into a field near the small French town of Annœullin, where loc
resident Cecille Deloffre found the badly injured pilot. Ball died the next day, and w
afforded a full military funeral by the Germans. He was only 20 years old. The Deloff
family still maintain Ball's grave, after honouring him by naming a town school and
street after him.

In February 1918, the War Office
.formed Captain Ball's father – a
.rmer Nottingham mayor – in writ-
.g that the German government had
.turned some of his son's personal
ems, which included a letter case
.ntaining photos and newspaper
.ittings, a cigarette case, a cravat
.n, 87 francs and a one pound treas-
·y note.

The Last Fight of Captain Ball.
(Painting by Norman Arnold)

Lauded as the greatest ace Britain
.s ever had, with 43 'kills' to his
.edit, Ball epitomized hope at a time
.hen Britain needed it most – a liv-
.g legend throughout the nation. For his unbridled gallantry, Ball became one of the
.ost decorated men of the Great War: Victoria Cross (VC) (Posthumous), Distinguished
.ervice Order (DSO) & Two Bars, Military Cross (MC), 1914–15 Star, British War Medal,
.ictory Medal and Mentioned in Despatches (oakleaf), Knight of the Légion d'honneur
.rance) and the Order of St George (4th Class) (Russia).

.olonel Sir Lancelot Rolleston KCB, DSO, TD

The South Notts Hussars assembled on Tuesday for their annual training, which is to
extend over a period of eleven days. The four squadrons met at their various centres as
follows: A (Bingham) at West Bridgford, B (Watnall) at Bobber's Mill, C (Nottingham) at
Ruddington Grange, and D (Wollaton) at Wollaton Park, at which places they partook of
lunch. They marched to the Forest, where the regiment formed up under the command
of Colonel Lancelot Rolleston.

(*Nottinghamshire Guardian*, Saturday, 13 May 1899)

.orn in 1847 at Watnall Hall – the family seat – a few miles north-west of Nottingham,
.ancelot Rolleston was educated at Wellington College in Berkshire and Christ Church,
.xford. In 1877 he was appointed to the office of High Sheriff of Nottinghamshire.

With the rank of lieutenant colonel in the South Nottinghamshire Hussars Yeomanry,
.id given the rank of captain, Rolleston was second in-command of the 3rd Battalion,
.iperial Yeomanry during the Anglo-Boer War of 1899–1902. The South Notts Hussars
.rmed the 12th Company in this battalion.

On 1 June 1900, the 3rd Battalion, Imperial Yeomanry, part of Lord Methuen's column
.i route from the town of Kroonstad in the Orange River Colony, encountered a Boer
.ommando eight miles from Lindley. With other Yeomanry battalions taking the right
.id centre of the Boer position, the 3rd Battalion was ordered to move wide round the
.iemy's right flank and come in behind him. The troops came under heavy artillery
.id rifle fire as they swept round towards a long, low ridge where the enemy had dug
. Seeing a convoy of British waggons captured by the Boers moving off, commander
.the 3rd, Colonel G.J. Younghusband, took three troops from his Yeomanry, to inter-
.pt the convoy. Heavy resistance was met, however, and in the absence of support
. push home his attack, Younghusband was compelled to withdraw at 2.00 pm, his

Colonel Sir Lancelot Rolleston
(Painting by Noel Denholm
Davis)

Yeomanry in South Africa,
Anglo-Boer War.

force badly mauled. The battalion suffered twenty-six killed, wounded and missir
Rolleston sustained serious wounds in the arm and side. His wife, Lady Maud, was al
in South Africa as a volunteer to nurse the wounded, so her husband was in good ca
Rolleston recovered and re-joined his regiment on active service. Rolleston was al
mentioned in despatches.

A justice of the peace for Nottinghamshire, in 1902 he was appointed a Companion of the Distinguished Service Order (DSO). From 1908 to 1912, Rolleston was Colonel of the Nottinghamshire and Derbyshire Mounted Brigade, Territorial Forces, during which tenure he was awarded the Territorial Decoration (TD).

In 1911, Rolleston was made a Knight Commander of the Order of the Bath (KCB), and remained a leading figure in Nottingham, where he was appointed Deputy Lord Lieutenant and High Sheriff.

In 1914, Rolleston was appointed Honorary Colonel of the South Nottinghamshire Hussars.

He was also very involved with the Boy Scouts for more than thirty years, finally retiring as county commissioner in the movement in 1940 at the age of ninety-three, being regarded as the oldest Boy Scout in the world. Rolleston died of a heart attack on 25 March the following year at his home, Watnall Hall.

Lieutenant Colonel Lawrence Arthur Hind MC

> We got to the German wire ... I was absolutely amazed to see it intact; after what we had been told. The Colonel and I took cover behind a small bank but after a bit the Colonel raised himself on his hands and knees to see better. Immediately, he was hit in the forehead by a single bullet.
>
> (Private Tomlinson)

Born in 1877 in Edwalton, a small village three miles south-east of Nottingham, Lawrence Hind was educated at Uppingham School. He read for a law degree at Trinity Hall Cambridge in 1899 before being admitted to the Bar in December 1902. He then practised law in Nottingham with solicitors Wells and Hind.

During his time at Cambridge, Hind won the middle-weight boxing championship, and for several years he was a well-known follower of the Earl of Harrington's hounds. While canvassing for his unsuccessful bid to be elected an MP, Hind rode his horse to get about.

Hind received his commission into the 7th (Robin Hood) Battalion, the Sherwood Foresters on 11 April 1900. He was promoted to captain in 1903 and temporary major in 1913.

In January 1915, with the reorganization of the battalion, Hind was given command of A Company.

Hind arrived in France in February 1915 and was wounded, together with 100 other

Lieutenant Colonel Lawrence Arthur Hind.

Entrenched Germans await
their enemy.

battalion casualties, at Zouave Wood, Hooge, during a German artillery barrage on
their newly dug trenches on 1 August 1915. Hind was initially admitted to the Liverpool
Merchants' Hospital at Etaples in France, for treatment to his head wound, after which
he was repatriated for recuperation in England. He subsequently returned to France in
October to re-join his battalion, now as the second-in-command. He had been promoted
to the rank of major in July that year.

In mid-May 1916, the battalion's much-respected commanding officer, Lieutenant
Colonel Arthur Brewill, was invalided home with exhaustion and stress from the rigours
of command, in particular, the strain of the fighting at Vimy Ridge. Hind was his successor, taking up 'the reins of command with vigour and determination at a very difficult
period in the history of the battalion'.

Hind's award of the Military Cross appeared in the London Gazette on 3 June 1916, after
having twice been mentioned in despatches for the courageous and exemplary manner in
which he conducted himself on the front.

As mentioned in Chapter Three, Lieutenant Colonel Hind was killed in no man's land
in the fighting around Gommecourt on 1 July 1916. His body was never found, so his life is
commemorated on the Thiepval Memorial, France. He was 38 years old. His name is also
inscribed on the Edwalton Alms Houses war memorial, Holy Rood Church war memorial
in Edwalton, High Pavement Unitarian Church war memorial and St. Peter's Church war
memorial in Ruddington.

Lieutenant Colonel Harry Hall Johnson MC, CIE

Born in Bingham, where his father kept the Vaults, Harry Hall Johnson began his military
career eighteen months before the outbreak of the First World War when he joined the
Border Regiment. Quickly proving that he was officer material, Johnson received his
commission, and during the conflict, he held the rank of temporary major, having been
promoted in February 1918 when he was also transferred from the Welsh regiment to
the General List. While serving with the Border Regiment, in June 1918, Johnson was
promoted to full lieutenant.

During the war, Johnson earned the Military Cross while fighting in France.

In November 1920, Johnson relinquished his commission 'on account of ill-health caused by wounds', and was granted the rank of major. He subsequently joined the Indian army.

Upon the completion of his army service, Johnson entered the diplomatic corps, and was posted to Waziristan as the assistant resident. In 1937, he drew the public's attention when, by 'sheer force of personality', he defused a volatile situation on the North West Frontier by winning over a large number of 'wild hillmen' to British authority.

Such an exploit brought distinction to the county of Nottingham.

The drama, played out in the mountain gorges of Waziristan, was a battle of wits between Major Johnson and the Fakir of Ipi, the firebrand of the frontier, who for months had been trying to rouse the tribes to a holy war against the British.

After days of intensive preparation, Major Johnson summoned to Miram Shah representatives of the Jirga (Council of Headmen of the Utmanzai Wazirs). These tribesmen occupied nearly all of North Waziristan and part of the Bannu districts. The headmen, who normally only knew the law of the hill, then heard the voice of authority. They were so impressed that immediately several tribal sections accepted unanimously his assurance that the Government had no desire to interfere with the Islamic religion, and, finally, all sections of the Jirga took the oath to combine to end the wave of unrest, and undertook to fight the irreconcilables if necessary.

(*Nottingham Evening Post*, Friday, 9 January 1942)

With the rank of brevet major, and as political agent, South Waziristan, North West Frontier Province, in June 1934 Johnson was appointed a Companion of the Order of the Indian Empire (CIE) in the king's birthday honours list.

Johnson was appointed consul general of the New Dominion and Kobdo, with residence at Kashgar in India, a post he held until his term expired in April 1941. Three weeks after his return from India, he was recalled to the army.

Early in January 1942, the 49-year-old Johnson was promoted to lieutenant colonel.

kh sepoys and NCOs,
d Indian officers,
rth West Frontier,
1935.

5. THE UNITS

45th (Nottinghamshire) Regiment of Foot, 'The Old Stubborns'

The 45th was originally one of seven new regiments raised in 1741 during Britain's war with Spain, titled at its formation Houghton's Regiment of Foot, the 56th. With the advent of peace in 1748, the regiment was retitled the 45th Regiment of Foot. By this time, the regiment had also seen service in Gibraltar and Nova Scotia.

From 1755, the 45th took up a ten-year tour of duty to Canada where, in 1748, the regiment fought at Louisbourg, earning its first battle honours.

Upon the regiment's return, it was posted to Ireland for a further ten years, before returning to North America where it fought in the American War of Independence, 1775–83.

In the space of two years, the regiment was decimated in various actions requiring it to return to England with a strength of less than 100. Billeted at Nottingham on their return, 300 men from the town volunteered to enlist in the regiment, but on condition that the monarch, George III, authorized the inclusion of 'Nottinghamshire' in the regiment's title.

Service at home ensued, broken only by postings to the West Indies in 1786 and 1795. On both tours of duty, the regiment suffered major losses in its ranks to disease.

English regiment of foot soldiers, 1815.

In 1808, following a disastrous attempt by the British to take by force Spanish territories on the River Plate in South America, the 45th was deployed to the Iberian Peninsula for the duration of the Napoleonic Wars. Playing a key role at the battles of Talavera, Buçaco and Badajoz, the regiment earned a significant number of battle honours to sew onto their colours: Roliça, Vimiera, Talavera, Buçaco, Fuentes de Oñoro, Ciudad Rodrigo, Badajoz, Salamanca, Vitoria, Pyrenees, Nivelle, Ortez, Toulouse, and Peninsula.

Upon the cessation of hostilities with France, the 45th returned to garrison duties in Ireland and England, before being shipped to Burma for the 1st Burma War, 1824–26, earning the battle honours 'Ava'.

In 1843, the regiment was split into 1st and Reserve battalions, the former posted to the Cape of Good Hope, while the Reserve Battalion was again deployed to South America in 1846 to defend Montevideo. The reserves then joined the 1st Battalion in South Africa, where the regiment saw service in the Kaffir Wars and the Orange River

pedition. The regiment was granted the battle honours 'South Africa 1846–47'. At this
ne, the regiment sought permission to incorporate 'Sherwood Foresters' into its title –
s was granted in 1865, by which time the 45th was on a posting in India.

In 1867, the regiment joined General Sir Robert Napier's punitive expedition against
yssinia, which, after a 300-mile march, resulted in the successful taking of the Magdala
ountain fortress.

The 45th's final postings as an independent entity took place in the 1870s, with deploy-
ents to Burma and India, before returning to England in 1878.

In 1881, the regiment was amalgamated with the 95th (Derbyshire) Regiment of Foot to
m The Sherwood Foresters (Nottinghamshire and Derbyshire Regiment).

th (2nd Nottinghamshire) Regiment of Foot, 'Lily Whites'

e 59th, covering Nottinghamshire and Leicestershire, was raised in 1755 for service in
land. The regiment was on station in Boston, Massachusetts, at the time of the outbreak
the American War of Independence, having been posted to North America in 1763. The
th, commanded by Lieutenant General John Owen, fought in the costly British victory
the Battle of Bunker Hill on 17 June 1775, in which it suffered such heavy casualties that
regiment had to return to England to replenish its strength.

At the start of the 59th's ten-year posting to Gibraltar in 1782, 'Nottinghamshire' was
corporated into its title, recognizing its association with the county. During the French
volutionary Wars of 1792–1802, the regiment was deployed in Flanders in 1794, but after
ear, it was sent to St Vincent in the West Indies, where, in 1796, they fought the Maroons –
caped African slaves from America – to lay claim to the island as part of the empire.

In 1804, the 59th, now back in England, recruited a second battalion in neighbouring
rbyshire.

In 1806, the 1st Battalion formed part of an invasion force to retake the Cape of Good
ope, which, now governed as the *Bataafse Republiek* – Batavian Republic – was a vassal

ttle of Bunker Hill, 1775.
inting by E. Percy Moran)

state of the French. Four years later, the battalion was shipped to India for four ye before serving in Mauritius and participating in the invasion of Java in 1811.

At the same time, the 2nd Battalion carried out two tours of duty in the Peninsu Wars, and a brief and abortive expedition to Holland. With the abdication of Napoleor 1814, the battalion was posted to Ireland, but was sent to Belgium the following year wl the French emperor escaped from Elba. In 1816, the 2nd Battalion was disbanded.

In 1815, the 1st Battalion returned to India for a fourteen-year stint, fighting in the Th Maratha War and the Jat War during their stay. After India, for the next twenty-odd yea the regiment was garrisoned in Ireland, England, Malta and the West Indies.

Following the First Opium War of 1839–42, the regiment was deployed to China assist with the enforcement of the treaty terms. They would form part of Anglo-Frer forces that captured Canton during the Second Opium War in December 1857.

The following year, the regiment was posted to South Africa, followed three years la by a six-year period of home service. The regiment's final foreign posting in its curr form, was for thirteen years to the Indian subcontinent, notably fighting at the Battle Ahmed Khel during the Second Afghan War of 1878–80 (see Chapter 3).

In 1880, the regiment returned home, where it was subsequently amalgamated with 30th (Cambridgeshire) Regiment of Foot to form The East Lancashire Regiment.

The change of identity, however, did not detract from the battle honours proudly bo on the regimental colours: Cape of Good Hope 1806 (1836), Corunna (1812), Java (18z Vitoria (1818), San Sebastian (1818), Nive (1818), Peninsula (1815 to the 2nd Battali to the whole regiment 1816), Bhurtpore (1826), Canton (1861), Ahmed Khel (1861) a Afghanistan 1878–80 (1881).

British camp on the Shagai Plateau shortly after the entrance to the Khyber Pass. (Photo John Bur

South Nottinghamshire Hussars

Originally formed as a volunteer cavalry unit in 1794, elements of the regiment first undertook foreign service during the Anglo-Boer War of 1899–1902.

In April 1908, the first line, 1/1st South Nottinghamshire Hussars was formed. As part of the Nottinghamshire and Derbyshire Mounted Brigade, the regiment served at Gallipoli. With the subsequent brigade re-designation to 7th Mounted Brigade in 1916, the following year the unit served in Salonika, and then Egypt where it was attached to the Desert Mounted Corps.

In 1918, the regiment left the brigade, was dismounted and retitled B Battalion, Machine Gun Corps with the 1/1st Warwickshire Yeomanry. Later that year, it was numbered as the 100th (Warwickshire and South Nottinghamshire Yeomanry) Battalion, Machine Gun Corps.

With the rapidly escalating demand for more troops on the Western Front, a second line regiment was formed in September 1914, forming part of the 2/1st Nottinghamshire and Derbyshire Mounted Brigade. In March 1916, the brigade was retitled the 9th Mounted Brigade.

In June, with the exception of twelve regiments, all second-line Yeomanry units in Britain were dismounted and converted to cyclists. The 2/1st South Nottinghamshire Hussars' brigade was retitled the 9th and then the 5th Cyclist Brigade.

A third line regiment, the 3/1st South Nottinghamshire Hussars, was raised in May 1915. Moving to Derby in September, the unit was affiliated to the 14th Reserve Cavalry Regiment at Aldershot. In October, the unit was posted to Ireland with this cavalry regiment, ultimately being absorbed the following year into the 2nd Reserve Cavalry Regiment at The Curragh. In the 1920s, in line with the realization that horse cavalry had become obsolete on the modern battlefield, the regiment became the 107th (South Notts Hussars Yeomanry) Brigade, Royal Field Artillery (RFA).

In the early days of the Second World War, the 107th Royal Horse Artillery (South Notts Hussars Yeomanry) comprised the 425th, the 426th and the 520th batteries. The regiment, now part of the 1st Cavalry Division, served in Palestine, Mersa Matruh, Egypt, Suez Canal, Tobruk, Tmini, Nile Delta, Sidi Bishr and Beni Yusef. The batteries were equipped with Mk IIPA and Mk IV 18pdr guns, 4.5" howitzers, 25pdr guns and Bren carriers.

In June 1942, disaster befell the regiment during the North Africa campaign, when virtually the whole unit was destroyed while providing a defensive rearguard action at the Knightsbridge Box, to cover the retreat of the British Eighth Army, during the Battle of Gazala. Allied casualties amounted to 50,000 and Tobruk fell, a major defeat, of which Churchill would say, 'This was one of the heaviest blows I can recall during the war. Not only were its military effects grievous, but it had affected the reputation of the British armies.'

The 150th (South Nottinghamshire Hussars) Regiment, RHA, was the second artillery unit of the regiment. Initially consisting of the 434th and 435th batteries, a third, the 520th, was added later in the war. Equipped with the new Mk II 25pdr, elements of the regiment participated in the June 1944 Allied European invasion at Normandy. The unit was disbanded in November 1955.

In 1947, in a reconstruction of Britain's territorial army, the 107th was retitled the 307th (RHA) (South Nottinghamshire Hussars Yeomanry) Field Regiment, Royal Artillery (RA), while the 150th became the 350th (South Nottinghamshire Hussars Yeomanry) Heavy Regiment, RA.

Left: FIRE! South Nottinghamshire Hussars, Europe, 1944–45. (Photo Sgt Carpenter)

Below: Royal Artillery firing 105mm howitzers. (Photo Ministry of Defence)

The 350th then consolidated as the 350th (Robin Hood Foresters) Light Regiment, R The 307 (South Nottinghamshire Hussars) Battery, is currently in the 100th (Yeomanr Regiment, RA, together with the 201 (Hertfordshire and Bedfordshire Yeomanry) Batte and 266 (Gloucestershire Volunteer Artillery) Battery. All batteries are equipped with t 105mm towed L118 howitzer.

The regimental colours bear the battle honours South Africa 1900–02, Hindenburg Line, ehy, St Quentin Canal, Beaurevoir, Selle, Sambre, France and Flanders 1918, Struma, cedonia 1916–17, Suvla, Scimitar Hill, Gallipoli 1915, Egypt 1915–16, Gaza, El Mughar, bi Samwil, Palestine 1917–18

erwood Rangers Yeomanry (SRY)

tially raised as the Nottinghamshire Yeomanry Cavalry in 1794, the regiment's early s largely mirrored that of the South Nottinghamshire Hussars Yeomanry, serving South Africa during the Anglo-Boer War and continuing in the First World War as unted cavalry split over three line regiments. Due to its seniority, however, the iment was retained as a mounted cavalry unit after the war.

At the outbreak of hostilities in 1939, the regiment was deployed to Palestine with the Cavalry Brigade. The following year, however, the regiment's horses were stabled for last time as the unit was converted to artillery, participating in the Western Desert ences of Tobruk and Benghazi.

n 1941, the regiment underwent further conversion, this time to armour. Assigned to 8th Armoured Brigade, the regiment was equipped with M3 Grant, M4 Sherman and sader tanks. In a theatre dominated by major clashes of armour between the Eighth my and the German Afrika Korps, the regiment invariably found itself embroiled in k battles in Alam el Halfa, El Alamein and Tunisia.

On D-Day, 6 June 1944, now equipped with DD (Duplex Drive) Sherman amphibious ks and the upgraded Sherman Firefly sporting a powerful 3" gun, the regiment – with British Second Army – fought out of France, through northern Belgium, and on to rman soil after the costly taking of Arnhem on the Dutch–German border. The regint earned 30 battle honours and 159 awards during the Second World War.

n 1967, the regiment was reduced in size and re-formed as a reconnaissance squadron the recently created Royal Yeomanry. For the next twenty-five years, the squadron was,

tish 5in medium gun in desert livery. (Photo Gerry van Tonder)

Alvis FV601 Saladin armoured car. (Photo Gerry van Tonder)

FV4034 Challenger 2 main battle tanks parked up during divisional exercises. (Photo Cpl Daniel Wiepen)

over time, equipped with Ferret and Alvis Saladin and Saracen armoured cars, followed by the FV105 Sultan Army Command and Control Vehicle, and the FV104 Samaritan Armoured Ambulance.

In 1992, the Sherwood Rangers transferred to become B Squadron, the Queen's Own Yeomanry, in the role of reconnaissance for Allied Rapid Reaction Corps (ARRC) within Allied Command Europe (ACE). The squadron operated Combat Vehicle Reconnaissance (Tracked) – CVR(T) – Scimitar and Sabre armoured fighting vehicles.

In 1999, the squadron re-joined the Royal Yeomanry as FV4034 Challenger 2 main battle tank (MBT) reserves. In 2006, the squadron adopted a CBRN (Chemical, biological, radiological and nuclear defence) reconnaissance role, operating the WIMIK version of the Land Rover Wolf.

7th (Robin Hood) Battalion, The Sherwood Foresters

The 1st Nottinghamshire (Robin Hood) Rifle Volunteer Corps raised by Adjutant Jonathan White on 15 November 1859, and simply known as the Robin Hood Rifles, was re-formed in 1881 to become the 3rd Volunteer Battalion of The Sherwood Foresters (Nottinghamshire and Derbyshire Regiment), comprising ten companies.

Following an exemplary tour of duty in South Africa during the Anglo-Boer War, in 1908, as part of a national restructuring exercise, the battalion was transferred to the Territorial Force and retitled the 7th (Robin Hood) Battalion, The Sherwood Foresters.

During the Great War, second and third (reserve) line battalions were raised. The 1/7th, having landed in France in February 1915 with the 46th (North Midland) Division, was thoroughly blooded at the Battle of Hohenzollern Redoubt, in which Captain Charles Vickers earned the battalion's first Victoria Cross. On 1 July 1916, the first day of the Battle of the Somme, four companies of the battalion attacked the German stronghold in the Gommecourt Salient on the northern extreme of the front, suffering catastrophic casualties.

At this time, the 2/7th was deployed to Ireland to assist with quelling the Easter Rising in Dublin in April 1916. Afterwards, this second line unit was shipped to the Western Front, where they saw action at Passchendaele and Cambrai. Early in 1918, to augment numbers, the 2/7th was absorbed by the 1/7th.

The battalion was briefly disbanded in June 1919, but re-formed with the restructured Territorial Army, or TA. In 1936, the Robin Hoods was converted into an anti-aircraft unit in the Royal Engineers, and retitled 42nd (The Robin Hoods, Sherwood Foresters) Anti-aircraft Battalion. The battalion was based in the West Riding area, as part of the 32nd (Midland) Anti-Aircraft Group, 2nd Anti-Aircraft Division.

Transferring to the Royal Artillery in a defensive role in August 1940, the regiment was retitled the 42nd (Robin Hoods, Sherwood Foresters) Searchlight Regiment, forming part of Derby's air defences during the Blitz on Midlands towns and cities in that year. With the Allied Normandy invasion pushing inland, the regiment landed in France to take up similar searchlight duties in north-western Europe. They spent time posted in Antwerp, assisting with the defence of the port from German V1 and V2 rocket attacks, gratefully acknowledged by Belgium awarding the Croix de Guerre to the regiment.

In 1947, the Robin Hoods were re-absorbed into the RA and retitled the 577th (The Robin Hoods, Sherwood Foresters) Searchlight Regiment, RA. Over the next two decades, the unit underwent several name changes, including, in 1955, an amalgamation

THE SURRENDER OF THE RAILWAY PIONEERS

Private James Brady, B Company, 4th Sherwood Foresters [Nottinghamshire], in a letter to his uncle, who resides in Havelock-street, Nottingham, written at Ladysmith on July 27th, says he has just recovered from the effects of the treatment he received at the hands of the Boers while a prisoner. He continues:

"On the 6th of July we were ordered from Zand River, where to, we did not know until we got to Roodeval Station. That done [set up camp], three sections of my company, B Company, were ordered to guard the station. All was well until about 3 a.m., when one of my 'pals' on guard saw a figure moving about 300 yards from where we were on guard.

I shouted with all my voice, 'Halt, who comes there!' No answer. The officer fired, but missed. We could see the fellow galloping for his life on horseback. At 5 a.m., we noticed a Boer coming in with a white flag. He halted 200 yards from me, and said he had a message. The orderly fetched it in. It said, 'We ask you to surrender. We have 2,000 men and six guns.'

Captain Gale replied, 'Certainly not.' And then 'goose fair' started.

There were only 68 of us men with the Railway Pioneers altogether. We were soon in fighting position, but I had scarcely got down when a poor old fellow named Ryan, of the Pioneers, was hit with a shell that killed him and Captain Gale, who was in command. I shall never forget the poor old fellow's moans and cries the longest day I live. I was giving him a drink of water while the bullets and shells were going 'ping-ping' all around me.

It started just after 5 a.m., and we were compelled to surrender, or be cut up. After surrender, came punishment for us. We were marched about the country like cattle, sleeping out on the veldt, when we got a chance to sleep.

The first ten days they gave us one and a half biscuits, and Tommy Strong could not have broken one with a 40lb hammer. We were living on Indian corn meal until we got to the Upper Tugela. A gentleman gave us a feed of dry bread and coffee. We were tramping day and night for 29 days. I walked over 40 miles with my socks on; no boots on, as my feet swelled and burst the laces.

We got released on the 5th of this month, and everything is all gay."

[The Goose Fair is a 700-year-old annual event in Nottingham, which, in 2015, offered 500 fairground attractions that drew 400,000 visitors in the five days it was held.]

(*Nottinghamshire Guardian*, Saturday, 25 August 1900)

with the 350th (South Nottinghamshire Hussars Yeomanry) Heavy Regiment, RA, and the 528th Light Anti-Aircraft Regiment (West Nottinghamshire) to form the 350th (The Robin Hood Foresters) Heavy Regiment, RA. The following year the title 'Heavy' was altered to 'Light'.

...tish 3.7in anti-aircraft gun. (Photo Gerry van Tonder)

British 90cm searchlight. (Photo Gerry van Tonder)

In 1961, the regiment moved to the Royal Engineers and was retitled the 350 (The Robin Hood Foresters) Field Squadron. In 1967, in line with further army structural reforms, the regiment returned to the Sherwood Foresters as part of The Robin Hood (Territorial) Battalion, a Territorial and Army Volunteer Reserve unit.

The regiment was again reduced in strength in 1969, becoming the Robin Hood (T Battalion, The Sherwood Foresters, Royal Engineers, falling under the wing of 73 Enginee Regiment, RE. In 1971, the regiment became D (Robin Hood Foresters) Company, 3rd (V Battalion of the newly formed Worcestershire and Sherwood Foresters Regiment.

In 1992, D Company became the Headquarters Company, effectively heralding the fin demise of the Robin Hood pedigree. In 1999, this company was also disbanded. The nam was previously used by A Company, The Nottinghamshire Army Cadet Force continued use the name until 2007, when they were retitled The Rifles.

The Robin Hood Rifles Cadet Corps of Drums is now the only entity left using 'Rob Hood' in its title. The corps teaches the playing of musical instruments and parade drill young people aged between 12 and 18 years 9 months. They perform at public events Europe and the UK, such as at the Last Post parade at the Menin Gate Memorial in Ypr and the Albert Ball VC annual commemorative service.

6. BARRACKS AND BUILDINGS

Nottingham Castle and Drill Hall

Today, little remains of the Norman castle sited on Castle Rock, its construction ordered by William the Conqueror in 1067. In the centuries that followed, successive monarchs utilized the castle as a focal point of their sovereignty in the English Midlands. As a consequence, however, it would also be a strategic and symbolic target for dissenters against the Crown.

The mid-twelfth-century monarch, Henry II, carried out extensive work on the bastion, constructing staggered baileys around the keep. At the end of the century, Richard I, the Lionheart, used force at the castle to quell an insurrection by his brother Prince John.

On a dark October night in 1330, Edward III with a group of loyal friends, gained access to the castle via a secret tunnel to 'dethrone' Roger Mortimer, usurper to the English throne. Mortimer, who in a conspiracy with Edward's mother, the queen consort Isabella, had overthrown Edward II and taken up residence in Nottingham Castle.

In his brief two-year reign, Richard III spent a great deal of his time in Nottingham Castle, and it was from here that he rode to his death at the Battle of Bosworth.

Charles I famously raised his royal standard at the castle as a Royalist military rallying point during the English Civil War. Parliamentarians, however, commanded by Colonel John Hutchinson, occupied the castle after the king's departure, retaining it as a Parliamentarian stronghold for the remainder of the conflict. Following the execution of

Nottingham Castle gatehouse, with parts of the earlier structure visible. (Photo Gerry van Tonder)

Charles in 1649, Hutchinson, determined that Nottingham Castle would never again be used in war, received parliament's permission to demolish the castle.

With the restoration of the monarchy and Charles II to the throne in 1660, Henry Cavendish, the 2nd Duke of Newcastle, constructed a 'ducal palace' on top of the castle foundations. In 1831, rioters protesting against the House of Lords veto of the Reform Bill, torched the palace, reducing it to a charred shell. A similar building was constructed.

Four decades later, the Corporation of Nottingham entered into a 500-year lease on the property. The palace, with some remodelling, was rebuilt and opened in July 1878 as a public museum to fine arts.

Just below and adjacent to the castle, once stood the Castlegate Drill Hall. Built in 1874, and serving one time as a riding school, the building was the headquarters of the Robin Hood Rifle Corps.

OPENING OF THE NEW DRILL HALL

On Monday, the capacious new drill hall for the accommodation of the Robin Hood rifles was opened. Two hundred men were put through the review exercise by Capt. White, adjutant of the regiment, and some new systems of firing exercise, originating from the War Office, were also gone through with a precision and smartness which elicited the approval of their able and experienced officer. The other officers present were Capt. Hunt and Lieutenant Hack, and when it is remembered that the members have not been drilled together since last Autumn, they showed great efficiency in the various movements.

The floor of the building is of asphalte [sic], and the whole structure is both extensive and substantial. The builder was Mr. Wright and the architect Captain Evans, who belongs to the Robin Hoods.

(*Nottinghamshire Guardian*, Friday, 17 April 1874)

The reconstructed Ducal Palace. (Photo Gerry van Tonder)

Derby Road Drill Hall

In November 1906, plans were drawn up for a new drill hall on a Corporation-owned site at 174 Derby Road, Nottingham. Having outgrown the drill hall on Castlegate, larger premises were required for the administration and training of two battalions of the Robin Hood Rifles. In addition to a hall which would accommodate 3,000, the four-storey building would provide rooms for headquarters' staff, officers and NCOs, band practice, quartermaster stores and an armoury. There will also be 'storage room for ambulances, machine guns, and the impediments necessary for camp. Two miniature ranges are to be provided, equipped with electric travelling targets'.

Upon the mobilization of territorials at the outbreak of the First World War, the Derby Road Drill Hall, now also headquarters to the 7th (Robin Hood) Battalion, The Sherwood Foresters, was the concentration point for the roll call on parade of the battalion on 5 August 1914.

Opened in circa 1910, the imposing red-brick and ashlar-dressed Baroque Revival building today provides office and private accommodation.

Towards the end of 1948, as part of a national consolidation of the Territorial Army, the decision was taken for the Derby Road Drill Hall to provide headquarters and administration offices for local TA units, both city and county.

rby Road Old Drill Hall. (Photo Gerry van Tonder)

Erstwhile Arnold Drill Hall. (Photo Gerry van Tonder)

Arnold Drill Hall

With a guard of honour provided by F Company of the 8th Battalion, The Sherwood Foresters, Lieutenant Colonel Henry Mellish officially opened the new drill hall on Arnold Hill Road on 2 May 1914. Measuring 90ft by 30ft, the double-storey brick building incorporated a miniature shooting range.

Typical of drill halls of the period, for many years the building also served the community, a venue for shows and entertainment, especially during the Second World War. In November 1948, alterations were made to the floor of the drill hall 'to make it suitable for dancing'. This was in pursuance of the army's desire to introduce more events into the life of the rank and file. At that time, it remained the headquarters of P Battery, 258 Light Anti-Aircraft (Mobile Regiment), Royal Artillery (TA).

The 'Old Drill Hall' as it has become known, now serves as premises for commercial and financial businesses.

Chetwynd (Chilwell) Barracks and the 'VC Factory'

Built for the Royal Army Ordnance Corps after the First World War, the Chilwell Barracks and Depot in Nottinghamshire was established on the site of the National Shell Filling Factory (No. 6), partly destroyed in a massive accidental explosion on 1 July 1918.

In August 1915, Godfrey Chetwynd, the 8th Viscount Chetwynd, was tasked with the designing, erection and management of a facility for the filling of artillery shells for the First World War. Situated close to the village of Chilwell, the factory used amatol – a blend of TNT and ammonium nitrate – to fill high-explosive shells of 60pdr and over.

Shell-filling line during the First World War. (Photo *The War Illustrated*)

Following extensive tests on the most proficient method of shell-filling, the bespoke plant was manufactured and installed, and large-scale production commenced in March 1916. By September, the 24-hour operation had filled a million shells.

Come the cessation of hostilities, more than 19 million shells had been filled, containing 120,000 tons of high explosive, with a total weight of around a million tons. Over and above this staggering figure, 25,000 mines were filled for the Royal Navy and 2,500 heavy bombs for the Royal Air Force.

It is said that almost every shell fired in the Battle of the Somme came from Chilwell, and, although there were seven other factories in production, Chilwell alone contributed 50 per cent of the national output. During its lifetime, the factory despatched 224,000 railway waggons of finished product, the record being set on 3 May 1918, when 436 waggons were loaded. Part of the complex included a 9-acre store, which on occasion stocked over a million shells, in addition to 100,000 empty shells, stencilled and ready for filling.

Notwithstanding strict safety practices in the high-security facility, nineteen explosions occurred in the history of Chilwell, but these were all defined as minor. In circumstances that still remain open to conjecture, on 1 July 1918, eight tons of TNT exploded, the sound of the detonation being heard twenty miles away. A total of 139 workers were killed and 250 injured. Of the fatalities, a mere 32 could be positively identified. The remains of the others were interred in a mass grave in St Mary's churchyard, Attenborough.

With a disregard for their own safety, hundreds stepped up to bring the fire under control and remove shells and material which might also explode. Mr Frederick Kellaway, Liberal MP and Parliamentary Secretary to the Ministry of Munitions, made a reference to the factory possibly being considered for the Victoria Cross. There was no precedent for this and no VC award ever materialized, but the name 'The VC Factory' stuck.

The mass graves in St Mary's churchyard, Attenborough. (Photo Gerry van Tonder)

The barracks and Royal Army Ordnance Corps stores came on line in 1919. During the Second World War, the garrison strength numbered 5,000, the facility now a massive store and vehicle depot, the latter including mechanical transport and armoured vehicles. By 1944 Chilwell had a million square feet of storage capacity, which would later increase with the addition of 2,500,000 square feet of outsourced storage. Downsizing was rapid when the war ended, and at the end of 1961, the last of Chilwell's eleven post-war sub-depots was shut down.

Army Department Constabulary on parade at the main gate to Chilwell Barracks, *c.* 1965. (Photo *Chilwell Garrison Jubilee Year*)

In 1995, the name of the barracks was changed to Chetwynd, in honour of the filling factory's director. It now became home to 49 (East) Brigade, until 2015 when the brigade was merged with the 7th Armoured Brigade, titled 7th Infantry Brigade and Headquarters East. Also stationed at Chetwynd would be 170 (Infrastructure Support) Engineer Group, the Nottinghamshire Band of the Royal Engineers, Reinforcements Training and Mobilisation Centre (RTMC), Nottingham Troop, 721 Explosive Ordnance Disposal Squadron RLC and 62–66 works groups, Royal Engineers.

In November 2016, the Ministry let it be known that the whole site would be shut down in 2021.

RAF Newton

Located seven miles from Nottingham, Royal Air Force Station Newton – RAF Newton – was built in 1939 and allocated to RAF Air Command's No. 1 Group. In July 1940, No. 103 and No. 150 RAF squadrons arrived at Newton, flying Fairey Battle light bombers and Vickers Wellington 1A and 1C medium bombers.

A year later the two RAF squadrons left Newton, and for the next five years until the end of 1946, the station accommodated No. 16 (Polish) Service Flying Training School, which provided basic and advanced training for Polish airmen serving with the RAF. During the war years, other units were also based at Newton: Ground Defence Squadron, No. 722 Ground Defence Squadron, No. 2722 RAF Regiment Squadron (formerly No. 722 Squadron), and Detachment, No. 2 Flying Instructors School.

From 1946 to 1958, Newton became the headquarters of No. 12 Group, Fighter Command. The station then became home to Technical Training Command for electronic fitters courses, followed by the RAF School of Education in 1972 and the RAF Police

War-time control tower, RAF Newton. (Courtesy Paul Francis)

Training School two years thereafter. Since then, at various times, Newton has been host to the Headquarters Air Training Corps and the RAF Police Dog School. The Nottingham University College Air Squadron and then the East Midlands University Air Squadron continued to fly at Newton until 2001.

The former station is now a designated private industrial estate, in which many of the buildings have been refurbished for use as office and storage space. The airfield itself has been given over to agriculture, while Nottinghamshire Police use parts of the site for crowd control and dog training.

Memorial Nurses' Home

After the First World War, the people of the city of Nottingham and Nottinghamshire subscribed to a plan to extend the city's General Hospital as a memorial to the 'sailors, soldiers and nurses of the city' – it is noted that the word 'airmen' was omitted – who lost their lives in the 1914–18 war.

Fronting on to Lenton Road, the three-storey red brick building was designed in Classical style by the local firm of Evans, Cartwright and Woollett. Owing to the site's close proximity to the castle, construction in certain areas proved problematic when thirteenth-century, six-feet-thick walls were discovered, being part of the original castle's outer bailey.

The new Memorial Home was opened by the Prince of Wales – future King Edward VIII – in 1923, providing 130 rooms for nurses. In 1927, a further storey was added, bringing the room total to 170. Nurses had to be single and be prepared to conform with near-Victorian

The former commemorative nurses' home. (Photo Gerry van Tonder)

house rules. Only those on their weekly half-day shift were allowed out at night, but even then there was a 10.00 pm curfew.

With the closing of the Nottingham General Hospital in 1993, the nurses' home was given the new name of Royal Standard House, situated as it is on the site where, famously, Charles I raised his royal standard in August 1642, effectively triggering the Civil War.

In November 1995, Grade II Listed status was conferred on the large building, which has since been converted to prestigious apartments.

7. FOR VALOUR

Awarded for 'most conspicuous bravery, or some daring or pre-eminent act of valour or self-sacrifice, or extreme devotion to duty in the presence of the enemy', the Victoria Cross, since its institution in 1856, is Britain's highest gallantry award, with precedence over all other medals and awards. This list, based on that on the memorial in the grounds of Nottingham Castle, is of the city's and county's elite recipients.

Private Robert Humpston VC (1832–1884)

2nd Battalion, The Rifle Brigade (Prince Consort's Own).
Victoria Cross citation, London Gazette, 24 February 1857:

A Russian Rifle Pit, situated among the rocks overhanging the Woronzoff Road, between the 3rd parallel, Right Attack, and the Quarries (at that period in the possession of the enemy) was occupied every night by the Russians, and their Riflemen commanded a portion of the Left Attack, and impeded the work in a new battery then being erected on the extreme right front of the 2nd parallel, Left Attack.

It was carried in daylight on the 22nd of April 1855, by two riflemen, one of whom was Private Humpston; He received a gratuity of £5 and was promoted. The Rifle Pit was subsequently destroyed on further support being obtained.

Notes: When he died on 22 December 1884, at his home in Nottingham, Humpston was given a pauper's funeral and buried in an unmarked grave in the Nottingham General Cemetery. This was to remain so until a local resident raised money for a headstone, which was unveiled in September 2007.

Abandoned defence redoubt, Siege of Sevastopol 1855. (Photo James Robertson)

Rifleman Francis Wheatley VC, DCM (1826–65)

1st Battalion Rifle Brigade (Prince Consort's Own).
Victoria Cross citation, London Gazette, 24 February 1857:
  For throwing a live shell over the parapet of the trenches.

Notes: On 12 October 1854, during fighting at Sevastopol, a live Russian shell landed in the British trench. After failing to disarm the shell with the butt of his rifle, Wheatley managed to manhandle the shell out of the trench, where it immediately exploded. No one was injured. He earned his Distinguished Conduct Medal the day before his VC action.

Captain William Raynor VC (1795–1860)

Bengal Veteran Establishment, Bengal Army.
Victoria Cross citation, London Gazette, 18 June 1858:
  For gallant conduct in the defence of the Magazine at Delhi, on 11th May, 1857.

Notes: At 61 years old, Raynor is the oldest recipient of the VC. With eight other men, Raynor defended the ammunition store from mutineers for over five hours. Realizing that no one was coming to relieve them, they blew up the magazine, killing many of the rebels as well as six of their own.

Massacre of officers by insurgent cavalry at Delhi', 1857. (*Illustrated London News*)

Private Samuel Morley VC (1829–1888)

2nd Battalion, Military Train.

Victoria Cross citation, London Gazette, 7 August 1860:

On the evacuation of Azimgurh by Koer Sing's Army, on the 15th of April, 1858, a Squadron of the Military Train, and half a Troop of Horse Artillery, were sent in pursuit.

Upon overtaking them, and coming into action with their rear-guard, a Squadron of the 3rd Seikh Cavalry (also detached in pursuit), and one Troop of the Military Train, were ordered to charge, when Lieutenant Hamilton, who commanded the Seikhs, was unhorsed, and immediately surrounded by the Enemy, who commenced cutting and hacking him whilst on the ground. Private Samuel Morley, seeing the predicament that Lieutenant Hamilton was in, although his (Morley's) horse had been shot from under him, immediately and most gallantly rushed up, on foot, to his assistance, and in conjunction with Farrier Murphy, who has already received the Victoria Cross for the same thing, cut down one of the Sepoys, and fought over Lieutenant Hamilton's body, until further assistance came up, and thereby was the means of saving Lieutenant Hamilton from being killed on the spot.

Notes: When he discovered that Murphy had immediately received his VC, Morley complained, and only after an investigation was conducted, was he presented with his medal.

Colour Sergeant Anthony Clarke Booth VC (21 April 1846–1899)

80th Regiment of Foot (Staffordshire Volunteers).

Victoria Cross citation, London Gazette, 24 February 1880:

For his gallant conduct on the 12th March, 1879, during the Zulu attack on the Intombi River, in having, when considerably outnumbered by the enemy, rallied a few men on the south bank of the river, and covered the retreat of fifty soldiers and others for a distance of three miles. The Officer Commanding 80th Regiment reports that, had it not been for the coolness displayed by this Non-commissioned Officer, not one man would have escaped.

Notes: Rallying a few soldiers on the south bank of the Intombe River, Booth covered the withdrawal of fifty troops, fending off Zulus over a distance of three miles, thereby preventing a total massacre.

Lieutenant Colonel William Thomas Marshall VC (1854–1920)

19th Hussars, British Army.

Victoria Cross citation, London Gazette, 21 May 1884:

For his conspicuous bravery during the Cavalry charge at El-Teb, on 29th February las in bringing Lieutenant-Colonel Barrow, 19th Hussars, out of action. That officer havin been severely wounded, and his horse killed, was on the ground surrounded by the enem when Quartermaster-Sergeant Marshall, who stayed behind with him, seized his hand an dragged him through the enemy back to the regiment. Had Lieutenant-Colonel Barrow bee left behind he must have been killed.

Notes: The action occurred during the Mahdist War in Sudan.

Captain Harry Churchill Beet VC medal group: L–R Victoria Cross, India Medal, Queen's South Africa Medal, King's South Africa Medal, British War Medal 1914–20, Victory Medal, Coronation Medal 1937. (Photo Gerry van Tonder)

Captain Harry Churchill Beet VC (1873–1946)

1st Battalion, Derbyshire Regiment.
Victoria Cross citation, London Gazette, 12 August 1902:

At Wakkerstroom, on the 22nd April, 1900, No. 2 Mounted Infantry Company, 1st Battalion Derbyshire Regiment, with two squadrons, Imperial Yeomanry, had to retire from near a farm, under a ridge held by Boers.

Corporal Burnett, Imperial Yeomanry, was left on the ground wounded, and Corporal Beet, on seeing him, remained behind and placed him under cover, bound up his wounds, and by firing prevented the Boers from coming down to the farm till dark, when Doctor Wilson, Imperial Yeomanry, came to the wounded man's assistance. The retirement was carried out under a very heavy fire, and Corporal Beet was exposed to fire during the whole afternoon.

Notes: The action occurred in South Africa during the Anglo-Boer War. Beet later immigrated to Canada, where, with the rank of captain, he served with Canadian forces during the First World War.

Sergeant Charles Ernest Garforth VC (1891–1973)

5th (The King's) Hussars.
Victoria Cross citation, London Gazette, 13 November 1914:

At Harmignies on 23rd August volunteered to cut wire under fire which enabled his squadron to escape. At Dammartin he carried a man out of action. On 3rd September, when under maxim fire, he extricated a sergeant whose horse had been shot, and by opening fire for 3 minutes enabled the sergeant to get away safely.

Notes: In August 2008, a commemorative headstone was erected at Wilford Hill Cemetery in Nottingham where, having been cremated, his ashes were originally scattered.

Wilfred Fuller VC memorial, Mansfield. (Photo Gerry van Tonder)

Corporal Wilfred Dolby Fuller VC (1893–1947)

1st Battalion, Grenadier Guards.

Victoria Cross citation, London Gazette, 19 April 1915:

For most conspicuous bravery at Neuve Chapelle on 12th March, 1915.

Seeing a party of the enemy endeavouring to escape along a communication trench, he ran towards them and killed the leading man with a bomb; the remainder (nearly 50) finding no means of evading his bombs, surrendered to him. Lance-Corporal Fuller was quite alone at the time.

Notes: He was also awarded the Cross of St. George, 3rd (Russia), specifically requested by the Russian Tsar.

Corporal James Upton VC (1888–1949)

1st Battalion, The Sherwood Foresters (The Nottinghamshire and Derbyshire Regiment)

Victoria Cross citation, London Gazette, 29 June 1915:

For most conspicuous bravery near Rouges Bancs on 9th May, 1915.

During the whole of this day Corporal Upton, displayed the greatest courage in rescuing the wounded whilst exposed to very heavy rifle and artillery fire, going close to the enemy's parapet regardless of his own personal safety. One wounded man was killed by a shell whilst this Non-commissioned Officer was carrying him.

When Corporal Upton was not actually carrying in the wounded he was engaged in bandaging and dressing the serious cases in front of our parapet, exposed to the enemy's fire.

Notes: The action took place during the Battle of Aubers Ridge, a British offensive on the Western Front.

Private Samuel Harvey VC (1881–1960)

1st Battalion, York and Lancaster Regiment.
Victoria Cross citation, London Gazette, 16 November 1915:

For most conspicuous bravery in "Big Willie" trench on 29th September, 1915. During a heavy bombing attack by the enemy, and when more bombs were urgently required for our front, Private Harvey volunteered to fetch them. The communication trench was blocked with wounded and reinforcements, and he went backwards and forwards across the open under intense fire and succeeded in bringing up no less than thirty boxes of bombs before he was wounded in the head. It was mainly due to Private Harvey's cool bravery in supplying bombs that the enemy was eventually driven back.

(Photo by Gerry van Tonder)

Notes: Harvey was also awarded the French Légion d'honneur (5th class) and the Cross of the Order of St George (Russia).

Sir Charles Geoffrey Vickers VC (1894–1982)

1/7th (Robin Hood) Battalion, Sherwood Foresters (Nottinghamshire and Derbyshire Regiment).
Victoria Cross citation, London Gazette, 16 November 1915:

For most conspicuous bravery on 14th October, 1915, in the Hohenzollern redoubt.

When nearly all his men had been killed or wounded, and with only two men available to hand him bombs, Captain Vickers held a barrier for some hours against heavy German bomb attacks from front and flank.

Regardless of the fact that his own retreat would be cut off, he had ordered a second barrier to be built behind him in order to ensure the safety of the trench. Finally he was severely wounded, but not before his magnificent courage and determination had enabled the second barrier to be completed.

A critical situation was thus saved.

Notes: Vickers was also awarded the Croix de Guerre (Belgium) in 1918. He was knighted for services during the Second World War as Deputy Director General at the Ministry of Economic Warfare, in charge of economic intelligence, and as a member of the Joint Intelligence Committee.

Private John Joseph Caffrey VC (1891–1953)

2nd Battalion, York and Lancaster Regiment.
Victoria Cross citation, London Gazette, 22 January 1916:

For most conspicuous bravery on 16th November 1915 near La Brique. A man of the West Yorkshire Regiment had been badly wounded and was lying in the open unable to move and

John Joseph Caffrey VC. (Ministry of Information)

in full view of and about 300 to 400 yards from the enemy's trenches. Corporal Stirk, Royal Army Medical Corps, and Private Caffrey at once started out to rescue him, but at the first attempt they were driven back by shrapnel fire.

Soon afterwards they started again under close sniping and machine-gun fire, and succeeded in reaching and bandaging the wounded man, but, just as Corporal Stirk had lifted him on Private Caffrey's back, he himself was shot in the head. Private Caffrey put down the wounded man, bandaged Corporal Stirk and helped him back to safety. He then returned and brought in the man from the West Yorkshire Regiment.

He had made three journeys across the open under close and accurate fire and had risked his own life to save others with the utmost coolness and bravery.

Notes: He was also awarded the Cross of St George (4th Class) (Russia).

Sapper William Hackett VC (Posthumous) (1873–1916)

254th Tunnelling Company, Royal Engineers.
Victoria Cross citation, London Gazette, 5 August 1916:

For most conspicuous bravery when entombed with four others in a gallery owing to the explosion of an enemy mine. After working for 20 hours, a hole was made through fallen earth and broken timber, and the outside party was met. Sapper Hackett helped three of the men through the hole and could easily have followed, but refused to leave the fourth who had been seriously injured, saying, "I am a tunneller, I must look after the others first". Meantime, the hole was getting smaller, yet he still refused to leave his injured comrad

Finally, the gallery collapsed, and though the rescue party worked desperately for four days the attempt to reach the two men failed. Sapper Hackett well knowing the nature of sliding earth, the chances against him, deliberately gave his life for his comrade.

Notes: The 43-year-old Hackett had been with a party working on the Shaftsbury Avenue Mine, Givenchy-lès-la-Bassée, France. His body was never found.

Captain Albert Ball VC (Posthumous), DSO and Two Bars, MC (1896–1917)

2/7th (Robin Hood) Battalion of the Sherwood Foresters (Nottinghamshire and Derbyshire Regiment), attached Royal Flying Corps.
Victoria Cross citation, London Gazette, 8 June 1917:

For most conspicuous and consistent bravery from the 25th of April to the 6th of May, 1917, during which period Capt. Ball took part in twenty-six combats in the air and destroyed eleven hostile aeroplanes, drove down two out of control, and forced several others to land.

In these combats Capt. Ball, flying alone, on one occasion fought six hostile machines, twice he fought five and once four. When leading two other British aeroplanes he attacked an enemy formation of eight. On each of these occasions he brought down at least one enemy.

Several times his aeroplane was badly damaged, once so seriously that but for the most delicate handling his machine would have collapsed, as nearly all the control wires had been shot away. On returning with a damaged machine he had always to be restrained from immediately going out on another.

In all, Capt. Ball has destroyed forty-three German aeroplanes and one balloon, and has always displayed most exceptional courage, determination and skill.

Distinguished Service Order citation, London Gazette, 26 September 1916:

For conspicuous gallantry and skill. Observing seven enemy machines in formation, he immediately attacked one of them and shot it down at 15 yards range. The remaining machines retired. Immediately afterwards, seeing five more hostile machines, he attacked one at about 10 yards range and shot it down, flames coming out of the fuselage. He then attacked another of the machines, which had been firing at him, and shot it down into a village, when it landed on the top of a house. He then went to the nearest aerodrome for more ammunition, and, returning, attacked three more machines, causing them to dive under control. Being then short of petrol he came home. His own machine was badly shot about in these fights.

Distinguished Service Order 1st Bar citation, London Gazette, 26 September 1916:

For conspicuous skill and gallantry. When on escort duty to a bombing raid he saw four enemy machines in formation. He dived on to them and broke up their formation, and then shot down the nearest one, which fell on its nose. He came down to about 500 feet to make certain it was wrecked. On another occasion, observing 12 enemy machines in formation, he dived in among them, and fired a drum into the nearest machine, which went down out of control. Several more hostile machines then approached, and he fired three more drums at them, driving down another out of control. He then returned, crossing the lines at a low altitude, with his machine very much damaged.

Albert Ball VC memorial, Nottingham. (Photo Gerry van Tonder)

Distinguished Service Order 2nd Bar citation, London Gazette 24 November 1916:
For conspicuous gallantry in action. He attacked three hostile machines and brought one down, displaying great courage and skill. He has brought down eight hostile machines in a short period, and has forced many others to land.

Military Cross citation, London Gazette, 25 July 1916:
For conspicuous skill and gallantry on many occasions, notably when, after failing to destroy an enemy kite balloon with bombs, he returned for a fresh supply, went back and brought it down in flames. He has done great execution among enemy aeroplanes. On one occasion he attacked six in one flight, forced down two and drove the others off. This occurred several miles over the enemy's lines.

Notes: Ball was the first three-time recipient of the DSO. He was also awarded the Légion d'honneur (France) and the Order of St. George (Russia). He was posthumously promoted to the rank of captain. (see Chapter 4)

Lance Corporal Walter Richard Parker VC (1881–1936)

Royal Marine Light Infantry, Royal Marines.
Victoria Cross citation, London Gazette, 22 June 1917:

Walter Parker VC.

In recognition of his most conspicuous bravery and devotion to duty in the course of the Dardanelles operations.

On the night of 30th April/1st May, 1915, a, message asking for ammunition, water and medical stores was received from an isolated fire trench at Gaba Tepe. A party of Non-commissioned Officers and men were detailed to carry water and ammunition, and, in response to a call for a volunteer from among the stretcher bearers, Parker at once came forward; he had during the previous three days displayed conspicuous bravery and energy under fire whilst in charge of the Battalion stretcher bearers.

Several men had already been killed in a previous attempt to bring assistance to the men holding the fire trench. To reach this trench it was necessary to traverse an area at least four hundred yards wide, which was completely exposed and swept by rifle fire. It was already daylight when the party emerged from shelter and at once one of the men was wounded. Parker organised a stretcher party and then going on alone succeeded in reaching the fire trench, all the water and ammunition carriers being either killed or wounded.

After his arrival he rendered assistance to the wounded in the trench, displaying extreme courage and remaining cool and collected in very trying circumstances. The trench had finally to be evacuated and Parker helped to remove and attend the wounded, although he himself was seriously wounded during, this operation.

Notes: He was permanently disabled by his wounds, resulting in him eventually being invalided out of military service in June 1916.

Sergeant Major Robert James Bye VC (1889–1962)

1st Battalion, Welsh Guards.
Victoria Cross citation, London Gazette, 4 September 1917:

For most conspicuous bravery.

Sjt. Bye displayed the utmost courage and devotion to duty during an attack on the enemy's position. Seeing that the leading waves were being troubled by two enemy blockhouses, he, on his own initiative, rushed at one of them and put the garrison out of action. He then rejoined his company and went forward to the assault of the second objective. When the troops had gone forward to the attack on the third objective, a party was detailed to clear up a line of blockhouses which had been passed. Sjt. Bye volunteered to take charge of this party, accomplished his object, and took many prisoners. He subsequently advanced to the third objective, capturing a number of prisoners, thus rendering invaluable assistance to the assaulting companies. He displayed throughout the most remarkable initiative.

Notes: The Welsh-born Bye lived and worked in Nottinghamshire as a coal miner. During the Second World War, he served with the Sherwood Foresters guarding POWs.

Sergeant William Henry Johnson VC (1890–1945)

1/5th Battalion, The Sherwood Foresters (The Nottinghamshire and Derbyshire Regiment).
Victoria Cross citation, London Gazette, 13 December 1918:

For most conspicuous bravery at Ramicourt on the 3rd of October, 1918.

When his platoon was held up by a nest of enemy machine guns at very close range, Sjt. Johnson worked his way forward under very heavy fire, and single-handed charged the post, bayoneting several gunners and capturing two machine guns. During this attack he was severely wounded by a bomb, but continued to lead forward his men.

Shortly afterwards the line was once more held up by machine guns. Again he rushed forward and attacked the post singlehanded. With wonderful courage he bombed the garrison, put the guns out of action, and captured the teams.

He showed throughout the most exceptional gallantry and devotion to duty.

Notes: He was also awarded the French Médaille militaire.

Corporal Harry Nicholls VC (1915–1975)

3rd Battalion, Grenadier Guards.
Victoria Cross citation, London Gazette, 26 July 1940:

On the 21st May 1940, Lance Corporal Nicholls was commanding a section in the right-forward platoon of his company when the company was ordered to counter-attack. At the very start of the advance he was wounded in the arm by shrapnel, but continued to lead his section forward; as the company came over a small ridge, the enemy opened heavy machine-gun fire at close range.

Lance Corporal Nicholls, realising the danger to the company, immediately seized a Bren gun and dashed forward towards the machine-guns, firing from the hip. He succeeded in silencing first one machine-gun and then two other machine-guns, in spite of being again severely wounded.

Lance-Corporal Nicholls then went on up to a higher piece of ground and engaged the German infantry massed behind, causing many casualties, and continuing to fire until he had no more ammunition left.

He was wounded at least four times in all, but absolutely refused to give in. There is no doubt that his gallant action was instrumental in enabling his company to reach its objective, and in causing the enemy to fall back across the River Scheldt.

Lance-corporal Nicholls has since been reported to have been killed in action.

Notes: Nicholls had in fact become a POW. While incarcerated in a camp in Poland, the German commandant presented him with his VC ribbon.

Rear Admiral Robert 'Rupert' St Vincent Sherbrooke VC, CB, DSO (1901–1972)

Royal Navy.

Victoria Cross citation, London Gazette, 8 January 1943:

Captain Sherbrooke, in H.M.S Onslow, was the Senior Officer in command of the destroyers escorting an important convoy bound for North Russia.

On the morning of 31st December, off the North Cape, he made contact with a greatly superior enemy force which was attempting to destroy the convoy. Captain Sherbrooke led his destroyers into attack and closed the Enemy. Four times the Enemy tried to attack the convoy, but was forced each time to withdraw behind a smoke screen to avoid the threat of torpedoes, and each time Captain Sherbrooke pursued him and drove him outside gun range of the convoy and towards our covering forces. These engagements lasted about two hours, but after the first forty minutes H.M.S. Onslow was hit, and Captain Sherbrooke was seriously wounded in the face and temporarily lost the use of one eye. Nevertheless he continued to direct the ships under his command until further hits on his own ship compelled him to disengage, but not until he was satisfied that the next Senior Officer had assumed control. It was only then that he agreed to leave the bridge for medical attention, and until the convoy was out of danger he insisted on receiving all reports of the action.

His courage, his fortitude and his cool and prompt decisions inspired all around him. By his leadership and example the convoy was saved from damage and was brought safely to its destination.

he Battle of the Barents Sea, German destroyer *Friedrich Eckoldt*. (Painting by Irwin J. Kappes)

The fallen hero. (Photo Gerry van Tonder, National Memorial Arboretum)

Companion of the Order of the Bath, London Gazette, 1 June 1953:
  On the occasion of Her Majesty's Coronation.

Distinguished Service Order citation, London Gazette, 28 June 1940:
  For daring, resource and devotion to duty in the second Battle of Narvik.

Notes: Sherbrooke was also awarded the King Haakon VII Freedom Cross (Norway). He was High Sheriff of Nottinghamshire 1958–59, and Lord Lieutenant for the county 1968–72.

8. LEST WE FORGET

For you no medals such as others wear –
A cross of bronze for those approved brave –
To you is given, above a shallow grave,
The wooden Cross that marks you resting there.

Rest you content, more honourable far
Than all the Orders is the ross of Wood,
The symbol of self-sacrifice that stood
Bearing the God whose brethren you are.

Lieutenant Cyril Winterbotham, Gloucestershire Regiment
killed in action 27 August 1916, a month after he wrote this poem

)th Regiment of Foot
fghan Wars memorial,
ottingham Castle.
hoto Gerry van Tonder)

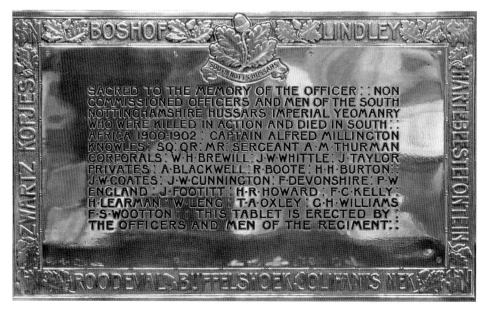

Anglo-Boer War memorial to the South Notts Hussars, St Mary's Church, Nottingham. (Photo Gerry van Tonder)

Anglo-Boer War memorial to the Robin Hood Rifles, St Mary's Church, Nottingham. (Photo Gerry van Tonder)

Anglo-Boer War memorial to the 1st Battalion, Sherwood Foresters (Notts and Derby), St Mary's Church, Nottingham. (Photo Gerry van Tonder)

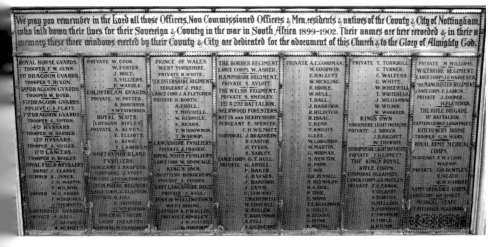

nglo-Boer War memorial to men of the county and Nottingham, St Mary's Church, Nottingham. hoto Gerry van Tonder)

Above: Captain Albert Ball VC memorial, Nottingham Castle. (Photo Gerry van Tonder)

Facing top: First World War memorial to the 17th Battalion, The Sherwood Foresters, Nottingham Castle. (Photo Gerry van Tonder)

Facing below: County employees' memorial, the Galleries of Justice Museum, Nottingham (Photo Gerry van Tonder)

Above: South Notts Hussars memorial plaque, St Mary's Church, Nottingham (Photo Gerry van Tonder)

Facing: Railway employees' memorial, Nottingham train station. (Photo Gerry van Tonder)

Trainee Pilot Andrew Gerrard Donaghy's grave in Gweru, Zimbabwe. During the war, Donaghy, who came from Newark, was one of hundreds of RAF personnel attending Rhodesian Air Training Group flying schools in the country during the Second World War. More than 140 such RAF trainees are interred in Zimbabwe having perished in air accidents. (Courtesy Mike Tucker)

ohn James died as a POW of the Japanese, remembered at Stapleford Cemetery.
Photo by Gerry van Tonder)

oth South Notts Hussars, Royal Horse Artillery, St Mary's Church, Nottingham.
noto Gerry van Tonder)

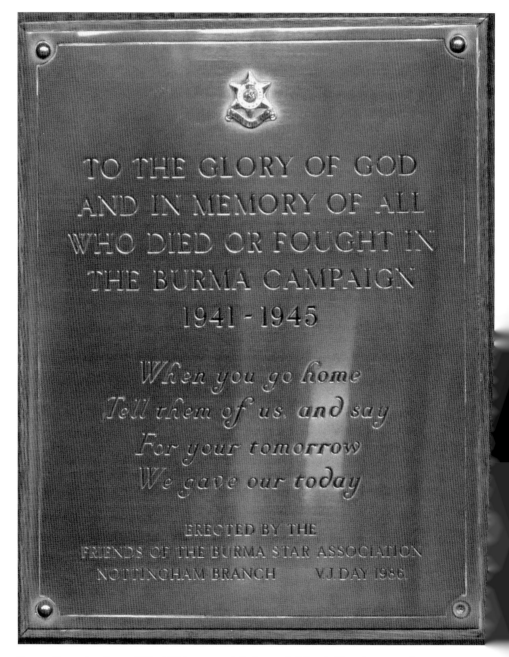

Burma Campaign Second World War memorial plaque, St Mary's Church, Nottingham. (Photo Gerry van Tonder)

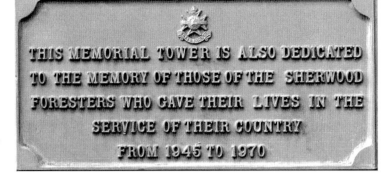

Sherwood Foresters memorial plaque 1945–1970, Mercian Regiment memorial, Crich. (Photo Gerry van Tonder)

Worcestershire and Sherwood Foresters Regiment memorial plaque 1970–2007, Mercian Regiment memorial, Crich. (Photo Gerry van Tonder)

Mercian Regiment memorial plaque 2007–present, Mercian Regiment memorial, Crich. (Photo Gerry van Tonder)

Mercian Regiment memorial, Crich. (Photo Gerry van Tonder)

ACKNOWLEDGEMENTS

My personal sincere thanks, as always, to the unfailing support from good friend, fellow historian and former brother-in-arms, Colonel Dudley Wall. Not only is his military knowledge of significant value, but his drawings and images of militaria from his private collection contribute a rich and unique element to my publications.

Thank you, Chris Cocks, for the production work on this book, and taking me along on the journey.

My thanks to Martin Bullick of East Midlands Trains for taking me into a cordoned-off building area at Nottingham's magnificent train station to access the Great War memorial to rail employees.

Source material has been drawn from The *British Newspaper Archive*, and the contemporary Second World War periodicals, *The War* and *The Illustrated War*.

The following publications proved very useful:

Brewill, Lieutenant Colonel Arthur W., et al, 'The Robin Hoods' 1/7th, 2/7th & 3/7th Battns. Sherwood Foresters (The Naval and Military Press Ltd., facsimile)

Dalbiac, Philip Hugh, *History of the 45th First Nottinghamshire Regiment, Sherwood Foresters* (Swan Sonnenschein & Co. Ltd., 1902).

Hammerton, Sir J.A., Ed., *A Popular History of the Great War*, Vol. 3 The Allies at Bay: 1916 (Fleetwood House, London, 1916)

MacDonald, J.F., *The War History of Southern Rhodesia 1939–45* (Rhodesiana Reprint Library, Bulawayo, 1976).

Brown, James Ambrose, *Retreat to Victory: A Springbok's Diary in North Africa, Gazala to El Alamein 1942* (Ashanti Publishing, Johannesburg, 1991).

Queen's Royal Lancers & Nottinghamshire Yeomanry Museum News, Issue No. 3 – September 2012.

ABOUT THE AUTHOR

Born and raised in Southern Rhodesia, historian, researcher, copy-editor and author, Gerry van Tonder came to Britain in 1999, settling in Derby, the city of his wife Tracey's birth. In Rhodesia, he completed 18 months' national service during the guerrilla war of the 1970s, before reading for a BA (Honours) degree at the University of Rhodesia. He served as a Liaison & Returning Officer during the Zimbabwean election of 1980.

Gerry has co-authored *Rhodesian Combined Forces Roll of Honour 1966–1981*, the landmark *Rhodesia Regiment 1899–1981* – a copy of this book was presented to the regiment's former colonel-in-chief, Her Majesty the Queen – and *North of the Red Line: Recollections of the Border War by Members of the SADF and SWATF 1966–1989*. He is author of *Rhodesian Native Regiment/Rhodesian African Rifles Book of Remembrance* and is working on a further Rhodesian title, *Operation Lighthouse*, an account of a paramilitary government ministry in the 1970s' insurgency. He has written three local history books: *Derby in 50 Buildings*, *Chesterfield's Military Heritage* and *Mansfield through Time*. For Pen & Sword he has written two Cold War titles, *Berlin Blockade: Soviet Chokehold and the Great Allied Airlift 1948–1949* and *Malayan Emergency: Triumph of the Running Dogs 1948–1960*, as well as *Nottingham's Military Legacy* and *Echoes of the Coventry Blitz*. Gerry has his own website www.rhodesiansoldier.com.

The author and a Rifles bugler at the National Memorial Arboretum. (Courtesy Colin Bewes)